God's People:
Instruments of Healing

Ottmar Fuchs

God's People: Instruments of Healing

The Diaconical Dimension of the Church

PETER LANG
Bern · Berlin · Frankfurt/M. · New York · Paris · Wien

Die Deutsche Bibliothek – CIP-Einheitsaufnahme

Fuchs, Ottmar:

God's people : instruments of healing ; the diaconical
dimension of the church / Ottmar Fuchs. - Bern ; Berlin ;
Frankfurt/M. ; New York ; Paris ; Wien : Lang, 1993
ISBN 3-906750-91-4

© Peter Lang, Inc., European Academic Publishers, Berne 1993

Printed in Switzerland

Contents

Preface

In summer 1991 I received an invitation from the University of South Africa, Pretoria, to spend several weeks as guest professor at the Department of Practical Theology in order to give lectures on the topic "The diaconical dimension of the church". I accepted the offer gladly and went to Pretoria in autumn of the same year.

What I have attempted in this book is to combine the lectures I gave at the UNISA with the enriching and critically rewarding results of the debates we had with each other in the department.

All of us have agreed that the future impact of the churches on the societies in which they are situated depends on how they are experienced as healing and solidarizing communities (concerning their religious and social praxis) within themselves and to the outside. Exactly this is the question of the diaconical dimension of the church: the question of how much love (in terms of mercy and justice) and freedom (to the individual and to society) are being spread by the churches in this world. That is to say, rigorously *in* (not above) the biographical and social, political and economic situation of the people in which the Christians and churches live and act, in South Africa as well as in any other country. Such an approach requires plurality because of the many different situations in different countries which need different decisions to be made for the sake of an actual increase of humanity and justice.

Theologically I refer not only to the biblical foundations but also to the latest theology of the II. Vatican Council (and of the appropriate understanding of the term "Evangelization") within the Catholic Church in which I have been brought up and where I live and work. I do not think that this theological position is something exclusive in the ecumenical sphere. It rather may support similar theologies emerging from other churches, as a kind of offer to solidarize with each other looking for the possibilities of substantiating our Christian faith.

My wish is that this book may encourage the Christians in all our churches and the churches themselves to seek and to find their theological and practical identities in the theme of the Women's World Day of Prayer in 1993: "God's people: instruments of healing".

I am deeply obliged to the interest and participation of the colleagues at the UNISA, especially to the head of the department, Prof Dr HCJ Pieterse, who not only had invited me but also looked after me extremely well during my stay in Pretoria.

I would like to include in my acknowledgments Mr Kenneth Wynne, without whose support in translating most of the original German texts this book would never have been possible to complete, Mrs Gertrud Böhnlein and Mrs Rosalinde Kohler, who both did such a good job to type the text first, then to alter it several times and to type the final version.

In spring 1991 I spent several weeks at the Lumko Missiological Institute near Johannesburg. There I took part in a pastoral course on the building up of "Small Christian Communities". On visiting several parishes in Soweto and in other townships I was deeply impressed by the vital connection of Christian spirituality and involvement for mutual help and justice. Much of that expressed in this book has been based on these experiences. I thank cordially the men and women who work in the Lumko Institute, especially P. Anselm Prior and Dr Oswald Hirmer for the many conversations on the way to the church, in which God's redemption fosters the liberation of the people from need and oppression.

Bamberg, March 1993

Ottmar Fuchs

1. Introduction

In preparing the following text I have restrained from the temptation to apply my concept to situations outside my own cultural and socio-political context. Such an application is entirely up to the readers themselves within their own contexts in which they live and work, according to the particular features and problems and to the necessary consequences. My own background is due to the situation in German society, where I have been living and working to date. I think it is the condition of any inter-cultural debate among equal participants that we invite each other mutually to St.Paul's words in 1 Thessalonians 5,21: "...but test everything, hold fast what is good."

1.1 *Personal*

Firstly, I would like to offer a glimpse into the development of my theological thinking according to the insight that there is no theological concept in general (even if claimed as such), because every theology has been facilitated *and* limited by the personal biography of the respective individual theologian.

Primarily, it was not abstract thoughts but concrete encounters with disabled, ill and disadvantaged people which made me and then my theological thoughts more radical and somewhat more intense than before. Therein was demonstrated something like the radicalizing power of unique experiences in our own biography. If a serious attempt is made to live in direct relationships and in encounters accompanied by risks (with the investment of time and devotion), then there are not only generative themes but rather generative encounters which cannot be quantified because one can not allow oneself too many of them if one does not wish to collapse. They can be regarded, however, in their quality as sources of life and as an experience of one's own limitations.

This has nothing to do with the false ideology of sacrifice or selflessness, but is based on the fact that such encounters have their own energy and resources and develop their own dynamic quality. Only in the singular (and never in general) do word and deed come together in human life. One's own ability to suffer and to show compassion does not develop abstractly but in the momentum of, in most cases, a few, deeper encounters of friendship and solidarity. Pastoral care over large areas is particularly well armed for flight from such intensity.

Not only the `Devil' but also God "is described in details". In real and unique fragments and details I find my place in belief and action. In the same way that the calling to Christianity is a fact of my own existence, so begins the connection between word and deed, between belief and change in the possibilities and impossibilities of my, in many respects, limited life. Similarly, encounters with people who help and care for others needing help and liberation have unearthed areas of life which have changed my theology and my definition of the church. The unconditional social welfare (diaconia, theologically speaking) for all those suffering demonstrates itself as an integral and practical part of the belief in God's unconditional love for us.

Let me at this point explain certain experiences in detail. Amongst my relatives there is a ten-year old girl who has an hereditary disease which can take many forms, from minor to severe disability. In her case one notices only minor speech difficulties and changeable behaviour. During the holidays she often spends a few days with me. On one of our walks in summer she told me of the horrors and the exclusion which she had experienced at school because her slightly brown skin pigment looks different and because she is at times more helpless and reacts differently than the others. She also told me of the worst insult exchanged amongst the other children at the time, which had also been applied to her, "You've got AIDS!" Then she said, "I'm not allowed to get married because I'm not allowed to have children because of the brown spots on my skin. But I've already got a boyfriend called Martin, whom I like very much!"

My blood froze with pain and anger at what this child had to endure. The worst is that I cannot do much about it because I have no direct influence on her life as such. Following this direct encounter with a "disadvantaged person" my theologizing became no longer arbitrarily diaconical but absolutely necessary. And the talk of evangelizing can only be effective if it has something to do with such people! For this reason I react increasingly strongly against any sort of theology (and this applies also to my own theological past) which comes along with generalizing boredom, without options and any "bite" and feels itself able to speak about every issue with nauseating balance and fluency. I have realized late enough that occasionally the question and silence are more important to me than the answer and speaking.

On a preparatory visit to the parents of a child taking first communion I arrived at the house of a working-class family. The father explained, "We don't have anything to do with the church, but we'd still like our daughter to take communion." In the lounge the sofa had been made into a bed. The father pointed to the grandmother and said, "We don't want to put Granny into care. She really needs caring for, but our family is large and we can take turns at looking after her round the clock." It was then clear to me that this family obviously does have something to do with the church because they are closer to the kingdom of God on a practical basis than some who preach the word of God in the church centres.

For a couple of years I was a minister in a parish where there was also the homeless shelter. One can therefore imagine the situation at our presbytery where the homeless regularly came to collect vouchers for food or sometimes money. We assumed that these men only wanted something from us and thus we treated them as objects of our willingness to help. That is, until something decisive happened to me. On this occasion I had more time than usual and started a conversation with one of the men, giving him an opportunity in which he himself could shed the facade of wanting something and tell something about himself. As I listened my shock grew and I noticed more and more that here was someone who, in his experiences with the church and mankind and also with God had something prophetic to say about Christ and the church. What he had to tell was and is important as criticism for both me and the church.

It would have been good if our church had had some communicative form in which this man could have told of his experiences. Through this encounter it was apparent to me that his story must be heard and appreciated in the Christian community and that such people from the "periphery" should be appreciated as important human beings because, due to their experiences of life, they have something decisive to say for those in the "middle" and are therefore indispensable for the comprehension of the Gospel.

Some time ago someone who had experienced the pitilessness of his own parish and its representatives in some particular way said, "I don't understand it. The Christians believe in a God of love, they claim to learn of God's love in the church and in the sacraments. But I ask myself where this endless love which they always have access to has gone? I have the impression that God's love simply peters out and disappears in the Christians and thereby for those outside who really need this love there's nothing left!"

The German Protestant Pastor Ulrich Bach, who himself is wheelchair-bound, tells the following story[1]: "A group of people in wheel-

---

[1] Cf. U. Bach, Kreuzes-Theologie und Behindertenhilfe. In: *Pastoraltheologie 73* (1984) 6 pp. 211-224.

chairs went swimming. Some of them are paraplegics. One or two of them are also incontinent. Which of their helpers went with them into the water? Karl and Susi went and the others said, 'Yuk! I couldn't do that.'" (This quotation as well as the following remarks will be dealt with in a primarily analytical-descriptive way; I do not wish to moralize on this issue). I know from my own experiences of several months of geriatric care in a hospital that the feeling of repulsion cannot be overcome in so short a time. The resistance is great and there are always limits to what a person can do. However, whoever restricts these limits from the outset with the "Yuk! reaction" of our so aesthetically sensitive contemporaries and does not work in himself on the possibilities of expanding these limits, denies this dimension of human existence and undermines his own ability to go beyond limits when it is necessary to experience the "negative side" of life and those who suffer in it. Then it is all the more difficult to allow or make contacts with these people which are helpful and liberating for both sides.

In this "Yuk!-reaction" we can observe the complete, attractive society which wants nothing to do with the "waste products" which it has mostly produced itself (as a result of traffic accidents, environmental catastrophes, accidents in the workplace, as a result of military action, drugs and medicine etc.). Similar examples can be found in the ecological field in wasteful production and the harmful treatment of its by-products. The same is also demonstrated in the repression and suppression of suffering and guilt. Our culture produces a feeling of repulsion which generates the constant behaviour of a healthy person and which makes it emotionally impossible for him to incorporate the negative sides of existence into the purpose of his life as well as his freedom and identity. The philosopher P. Sloterdijk put it this way: "The relationship which is drummed into people about their own excretion supplies the model for their treatment of all the waste products of their lives", that is, for their treatment of all negative experiences of weakness, baseness and embarrassment because they only accept that which is generally recognized, plausible and understood. In contrast one must now, "philosophically speaking, reconsider the usefulness of the useless and the productivity of the unproductive, realize the positive of the negative and recognize our responsibility for the unintentional".[2]

In my experiences living for some months with disabled people in a centre for spastics in England there were two qualities above all

---

2   P. Sloterdijk, *Kritik der zynischen Vernunft*, Vol. I (Frankfurt/M. 1983) pp. 288–289.

which made a lasting impression upon me as more intensive encounters; one was individuality, the other was the crossing of barriers. Due to the stigma and their life because of it, disabled people have a uniqueness and originality which is seldom found amongst their grey, uniform contemporaries. Their unrestricted openness to cross "normal" boundaries in encounters of physical contact creates relationships which foster deep emotional bonds on both sides. And how much richer our interpersonal contacts would be if we could incorporate both these dimensions into our "normal" world. I also learnt something else; many of them are at first difficult to understand. Impatient people give up after the first empathetic attempts and increasingly nod and say, "Yes, yes" without having understood a word. They do not invest the time nor the trouble to appreciate the physical difficulty and the ability of the disabled voice; how the words are formed slowly and with difficulty and are then uttered with a voice that is the expression of the whole body. One can understand them then and experience their words in a new way if one appreciates the corporeality of their voices and does not dismiss them too quickly because of initial difficulties and thereby, which is worse still, treat as unimportant that which the disabled person wants to say.

1.2 *Uneasiness*

Whereas increasing numbers of non-religious people in modern society today see the church's central duty and right to existence in its social welfare capacity, diaconia takes a marginal position in the consciousness of the church, its pastoral care and its forming of communities. The "essence" is seen to lie in the sermon, the sacraments and services as well as in the confirmation of one's belief in Bible-reading groups and discussions. This can be demonstrated empirically in the fact that Christians who are both close as well as more distanced from the church associate such words as "priest", "church building" and "service" and perhaps "religious education" with the central term "church". Very rarely would they link organizations and initiatives with the term "church" in which Christians are working together to help the disadvantaged and to liberate the oppressed and are fighting for their right to equality. The latter are obviously perceived as the active territory or consequence of the church and pastoral care and thus as the application of the essence of the church (and not as the essence itself).

Even if the active members of the church and the priests of our parishes were asked: "What is the most important factor in being a

Christian?" the answer would often be: "That one believes in God; that one believes in Christ!" The parishes are the places where Christian belief is preached in the sermons and the sacraments and where (if it is a particularly active community) the believers learn to discuss their belief with one another. On one level that is acceptable and is necessary for the identity of the church.

But still, when we look at Jesus himself and his way of preaching the Gospel we cannot help but feel an intensive uneasiness. There are too many stories and parables of Jesus in which it is surprisingly clear that when he speaks of the Gospel and the kingdom of God then he has already acted in a redeeming and helping way. So he releases people from destructive obsessions and identifies this deed with the arrival of the kingdom of God (cf. Lk 11, 20).

For Jesus, the love of God and the love of one's neighbour through to the love of one's enemies are processes which at the same time and level condition and elucidate one another. This is displayed in his words, his stories and his whole life. It is this practical reality which adequately explains his teaching.

These few brief introductory comments show that to be a Christian is not exhausted in the communal profession of the formulated truth of the Gospel nor in an intellectual acceptance of the true "Christian philosophy of life". Rather it shows its own and deepest foundation and motivation in the following of Jesus and thereby in the practice of love and liberation. Naturally, confession, songs, prayers and liturgy remain imperative, but they only attain their importance for real life and their existential meaning – as with Jesus who is indeed the expression of God's word – in the necessary connection with the concrete execution of the orthopraxy, in beneficial actions and encounters for and with each other. If one establishes the identity of the church based on the praxis of Jesus then the central issue is not primarily the unity of those who are already in its milieu and in harmony with its views. The important factor which usually creates not very much harmony is the tension-filled and risky inclusion of the weak, the needy and the oppressed. Precisely such an action fulfils Jesus`s proclamation of God's kingdom, also (characteristically!) against the objections of his disciples (cf. Mt 19,13, the story in which Jesus encounters the children).

Jesus did not allow himself any talk of God without redeeming and liberating encounters, without helping and actions of solidarity. This means for us that without such a praxis orientated towards Jesus the belief in Christ is "in a state of limbo", as God's love for us is only maintained in preaching and celebrated in the liturgy. As if God did not have anything to *do* with the love of mankind by becoming a human being himself.

To perceive and realize diaconia as the love for one's neighbour and as undivided justice, in the most serious cases of human and lifesaving contact with the suffering and oppressed as well as solidarity with the affected and those who care for them is a matter of great urgency considering the places of fear in the world and the areas of need in our societies. If the Christian interpretation of God takes place mainly at the horizon of interpersonal social welfare, then the realization comes gradually that God's connection with mankind can be experienced itself as diaconia, as his redeeming and forgiving treatment of the people. The preaching of God has therefore itself a quality of social responsibility, otherwise it creates, as knowledge imposed from above, more oppression and fear than it actually helps. We know well enough how often the Churches' preaching of God has caused terrible fears of him and his hell-threatening message!

The theological discussion concerning diaconia (social welfare) has become more intensive in the last decade in a (small) part of the academic practical theology in Germany and in the church's charitable organizations. This subject with these particular discussion partners is gradually blossoming as the current key subject of church praxis and practical theology.[3] It is expected from this "key" that it will do no less than open the door to the active building of communities for the sake of the victims of need, illness and violence and open the door to a committed "theology of liberation" in our country. This process promises much good because it has an "insistent connection"[4] with the real existence of the suffering and rescues the church and theology from a "self-fulfillment" only for the sake of themselves. Otherwise the church would not bear witness to the "Christ who lives in the present".

As in the Latin American Liberation Theology (for the sake of the poor), there is the development of a basic perspective which is interested in social factors. This is a basic premise and a basic decision searching for a concrete and acutely necessary humanity; in short, an option which places the church and theology under a definite criterion, in-as-much as they are able to be criticized on the level of

---

3   Cf. K.-F. Daiber, *Diakonie und kirchliche Identität* (Hannover 1988); O. Fuchs, *Heilen und Befreien* (Düsseldorf 1990).

4   Cf. H. Wagner, Ein Versuch der Integration der Diakonie in die Praktische Theologie. In: *Pastoraltheologie 72* (1984) 4 pp. 186-194, p. 189.

their actions. Free floating forms of praxis and theological conception which are concerned with matters (which are also important) such as an amenable liturgy and an active core-parish will be controlled because they have to present themselves to be judged by "diaconia" as a form of "acid test", to admit their responsiblity and to examine their relevance. The more I concern myself with this subject and come into contact with those who work professionally (particularly in charitable organisations) or on a voluntary basis with those affected, the more I sense that something like an imminent "Putsch attempt" is coming which will turn the Western praxis of the church and theology inside out and so "overthrow and leave empty-handed" some of the "dominating" main themes and figures (cf. Lk 1,28-53). I would like to join this process; in the search for an appropriate theological perspective and thus for a more effective organization of praxis in the urgent case of diaconia for the affected.

I prefer here to explain the term "affected". It is not a term belonging to the hazy subjectivistic (and therefore arbitrary) jargon of being affected or concerned but should be understood as a real objective collective term for all people who are affected by unhappiness, need, illness, oppression and fear. What is not meant (at least primarily) are those who are affected by the sorrow of affected people, but those people who are directly affected themselves. It is of course necessary that being affected also affects others, but more than just being affected is necessary and besides, one does not necessarily need this vocabulary which at least in its use to date smacks of individualizing edification and in the context of group dynamics has at its centre more those affected by the affected, than the affected themselves. The "good, old" words such as mercifulness, compassion and justice still provide as before a more precise meaning.

To establish those who are affected does not lie moreover primarily in the arbitrary nature of the emotional experiences of those not affected but in the demands for help and liberation of those affected themselves. The "self-evidence" of being subjectively affected can be misleading and can draw attention away from the decisive factors when it does not concern itself centrally with the sober empirical and analytical evidence of the determination of need and being affected (and then of course not only the need of others but of oneself). "Being affected" is only then a theological category if it means mercifulness which is directed towards those affected and if it comprises the praxis of God as an advocate for those affected (cf. Lk 2, 19; 7, 13; 10, 32; 24, 32); for the sake of the Gospel for the benefit of mankind and for the sake of mankind for the

benefit of the reality which Jesus calls the kingdom of God.

1.3 *Church for Other People*

In a time when coming generations must fear
that their death will coincide with the
"apocalypse", with the collective death of mankind, where therefore the future kingdom of
God is plausible as a catastrophic break into history, Christian hope can no longer easily speak
out in favour of a lineal continual transition of
present history into the kingdom of God (in the
form of worldwide ecologic and ethical progress) without not only supplying the hope for
this "improvement of the world", but also preparing itself as quickly as possible for corresponding active changes. Then it is all the
more important to learn in exact detail about
the socially unjust conditions from those pre-
sently affected, as a highly necessary basis for the
solidarity, and to act now with a view to the
future potential victims and as a responsiblity to
these people to undertake everything possible
which may prevent the collective death of
mankind. Since whoever says, "what happens
to my neighbour does not interest me" will also
say, "It doesn't matter what happens after I'm
gone!" The condition for the creation of the

necessary political majorities and national structures for action, so that such majorities come to being, is solidarity with the closest and most distant affected people of the present. Thus the integral paradigmatic change mentioned above will be complete.

If the church realizes its own identity for the sake of social welfare and justice towards the outside as well as inside for the benefit of Christians and mankind as a whole, then it will discover its goal as it assists in making possible, struggling for and forming the more humane future of mankind. The church can then refrain from its recruitment strategies towards the formation of a "club-like" identity.

Let me put my theses into the words of a German Protestant theologian whom I admire very much, Dietrich Bonhoeffer, who was killed by the Nazis because of his resistance against violence and oppression: "The Church is only the Church when it is there for other people". Bonhoeffer's assertion sounds resolute and provocative, especially if we think what its negation would be: the Church is not the Church if it is not there for other people, if – we might go on to say – it is there only for its own sake, merely as an in-group of believers with the appropriate ideological self-certainties and institutional structures, which then determine the character of the Church's social forms.

'Existence for other people' is different. It definitely (also) means the people who really are 'the others' – all the people who do not belong to the Church, as an institutional and doctrinal community of faith. It means especially the people who – according to the faith and morals which the church approves – count as unbelievers, sinners, outsiders, aliens. The Church is there so as to be there for these 'others': so as to expand the opportunities of living open to them and the quality of their lives. And it has to do this through direct, helping and liberating encounters and groups, as well as by way of humane social structures and just economic conditions.

This is the Church's task, formulated in general terms. But it catches light in the real and specific places where these 'others' are suffering, the places where they are living in poverty and need, despised and oppressed, in unjust conditions, or where their very lives are threatened. These 'ignition points' are not matters of choice. They are the places where the ministries of the Church are necessarily deployed. The Church, that is to say, is only the Church when it helps those who need help, and helps the helpers to help, and when it liberates the oppressed and helps the liberators in their task of liberation: and all this irrespective of who these 'others' are. This is the praxis in which the Church is authentically the Church, because its identity comes into being through service.

For the well-disposed, this perhaps sounds so obvious that its explosive quality, as criticism of the Church, may not at first appear, or be grasped. Yet here nothing less than the Church's identity per se is in question. For here service for others is made the decisive criterion for distinguishing in the Church's praxis between its maintaining of itself as an institution and its solidarity with others; between faith and ideology; between love and rule; between liberation and domination; between Baal and Yahweh – ultimately between godlessness and trust in God, or between anti-Christian conduct and discipleship. We sense especially that this touches the very nerve-centre of the Church's self-development structures when we observe the history-long ambivalence of its defence of the faith and its defence of its own institutions, seeing these things critically against the background of unconditional service – which means service not hindered by inhibiting conditions.

1.4 Neighbourly Love in the Church and its Limitations

Let me go back briefly to the beginning of the Church-History. As the Christian churches grew, it was their inestimable achievement, on the basis of a new religious unity, to cross frontiers in their own social spheres. These frontiers had hitherto seldom been infringed; and some of them – religious, ethical, political and socio-cultural – were heavily charged with restrictive sanctions. Yet, as the Church increasingly constituted itself as a group and formed its social identity, it inevitably created new dividing lines between what were now Christian congregations and their non-Christian environment. Here the development of the concepts 'heathen' and 'heresy' is significant.[5] There were certainly already movements running counter to this trend in the New Testament writings, and among early Christian theologians – writers who stress love of one's enemies, or uncondi-

---

5 See N. Brox, Häresie. In: *Reallexion für Antike und Christentum* (Stuttgart 1950-) VIII, pp. 248-297; C. Colpe, Die Ausbildung des Heidenbegriffs von Israel zur Apologetik und das Zweideutigwerden des Christentum. In: R. Faber and R. Schlesier (ed.), *Die Restauration der Götter* (Würzburg 1986) pp. 61-87.

tional service for all who suffer.[6] Yet we can detect an apparently ever-more dominant narrowing down of the universal character of neighbourly love to that of brotherly love within the Church.[7] Service for others finds its scope mainly within the limits of the new communities.

Of course there is nothing to be said against mutual service in and among Christian congregations. Only it is then easy to lose sight of the fact that there are people outside the Church who are not only in need of redeeming faith, but who also require help in their distress, and liberation from oppression. This aspect of the Jesus of Nazareth about whom the Gospels tell, recedes into the background, while doctrinaire apologetic and institutional demarcation lines between Christians and heathen, or between Christians and Jews, push themselves all the more to the fore.

In the first three centuries the minority status of the Christian congregations, and the occasional oppression they suffered, may serve

---

6 See P. Hoffmann, Tradition und Situation. In: K. Kertelge (ed.), *Ethik im Neuen Testament* (Freiburg 1984) pp. 50-118; M. Puzicha, Zur Aufnahme der Fremden in der alten Kirche. In: O. Fuchs (ed.), *Die Fremden* (Düsseldorf 1988) pp. 180-183.
7 See Brox 'Häresie' 255ff.; J. Becker, Feindesliebe-Nächstenliebe-Bruderliebe. In: *Evangelische Ethik* 25 (1981) pp. 1,5-18, esp. 10ff., 16ff.

as an excuse for this development. But after the change of conditions under Constantine, this no longer applies. The Church was now on the way to becoming a majority with a share in state power; and it was precisely as its influence increased that the frontiers between Christians and heathen were drawn more strictly, against the background of the new conditions of power. As a result, non-Christians increasingly experienced their dissident status in the form of defamation, discrimination and maltreatment.[8] Christians and the Church ceased to be aware, spiritually, theologically and ecclesiologically, that this kind of conduct towards 'unbelievers' was a slap in the face for the universal ministry, depriving the transmission of faith of its essential communicative basis, replacing it by an improper (because unchristian) more or less forced indoctrination and a press-gang type of integration. From here, not much stands in the way of developments in the Church's history leading to the 'wars of religion', pogroms and 'Christian' colonisations.

Here a contemptuous totalitarian ideology stands as unspoken sponsor: unbelievers do not deserve humane treatment – or deserve it less than believers. Consequently it is easier to accept the sufferings of non-believers than the

---

8   See Colpe 'Heidenbegriff' pp. 72–82.

bitter experiences of Christians. Furthermore, it is even legitimate to increase the sufferings of unbelievers, through pain and oppression, since they really deserve nothing else, or in order to bring them at last to true faith. To put it in somewhat vulgar terms: people may surely be forced for their own good 'to get to heaven'. The unbeliever can easily avoid suffering of this kind if he will only let himself be told what the truth is, and enter the fold of the Church.

The ministering love of the Christian God is radical in its universality. It is wide open. This God loves human beings as sinners without any conditions, and desires their salvations even before they change their ways (cf. Rom 5,8 and 1 Jn 4,10). But this love is obscured if the ministering love of Christians is dependent on the condition that the "sinner" must first of all enter the institutional and ideological fold of the Church, and adopt the good behaviour bound up with that. Christians and the Church would, however, be preaching the Gospel to themselves if they spelled out the 'limits' of their faith by *tearing down* the limits on their loving service for all. The persecuted Jews and the Communist in the concentration camp, the AIDS-infected homosexual and the slandered man or woman seeking political asylum – all these people belong to the social domain of the Christian Church and its charitable service, and to the sphere of its political solidarity, simply because they claim help and need liberation. This prevents the mentality which is seriously prepared to help only if certain moral, ideological or institutional conditions are fulfilled.

2. In the Beginning: Word and Deed

2.1 *The Experience of Meaning*

I would like to begin with some socio-linguistic deliberations concerning the relationship between word and meaning. When a young child learns to say "mama" then this happens in the context of certain particular encounters where the mother behaves in a certain way with the child and gives this process a name; "mama". Therefore from the beginning, the meaning of a word is defined in the context of certain experiences by actions with which it is used and learnt. Even when in advanced stages of learning vocabulary and of linguistic structures the power of abstract thinking increases to connect the same words with different concrete individuals (other children also have mamas and they all look different), the child does not lose the deep-rooted "case history" of his unique own mother and the linked learning process for this term (with all its ambivalent power). How mothers with other children are and look is learnt in encounters with these themselves.

The enormous achievement in learning a language lies in the combination of the abstract and the concrete; the term "mama" can be used for all mothers, even when they are all different and even contradictory. For the mothers of other children there is no separate word in the linguistic system because the term "mother" means all women with a child or children. The term "mother" on its own does not go into details concerning which mother is meant. To which particular mother this term relates is not defined by the word, but, for example, by an additional pointing phrase such as my mother or John's mother etc. The speaker refers to a particular person and evokes the corresponding concrete experience.

These simple considerations already make clear that there are two definitions of a word, the lexical meaning within a language system (mother is a woman who has a child or children) and the referential definition which refers to a particular mother "outside" of the language system. The meaning is only unambiguous in practice when the speaker combines the word with a concrete person or real facts. The latter case can happen in two ways: in the connection of the word with a story about the concrete person or in connection of the word with reality itself (for example, with reference to a personal or factual process which is happening in direct experience). The latter happens relatively rarely unless one happens to have a photograph or film in one's pocket. In linguistic communication we mostly have to rely on naming the actual subject in speech itself; namely through description or narration. This involves a high power of differentiation, namely between the one or other realization of the same word. This happens for the benefit of communication and creates understanding and a connection to reality.

The relationship described above between word and reality is applicable to all areas and levels. Such great words as justice and freedom, which are used by everyone, are only defined by the reality connected with these words. The freedom of which dictators speak is different from the freedom which is used in a situation of democracy. Although such words have a quality of automatic agreement (everyone is in favour of them) they do not express much if their universality is not reduced by the fact that the speaker can convincingly enough describe and relate that which he actually supports.

For example: in the discussion of peace relating to the "maintenance of peace", two completely different concepts of action are displayed, on the one hand, armament, on the other disarmament, both for the sake of security. A term does not only and primarily attain its meaning by the fact that its quality is abstracted and defined in our thoughts but by the fact that one can refer to a reality or an action and can say, "Look how I do it and how the others do it or what the conditions are and how the relationships are structurally controlled, that's what I mean when I talk of freedom or peace!" Only then do the differences and contradictions of the discussion partner become apparent. And only then does one no longer argue about "fictitious" phenomena ("ideologies") but about the formation of real existing relationships.

To understand a term one must reduce it to its material or communicative components. Only when I can say that, and how a word is linked with a particular action, does the word achieve a dimension of meaning which describes the praxis.

To avoid possible misunderstandings I wish to make clear at this point that the use of the term "action" here does not exclusively mean active behaviour but refers to human intentional actions as a whole,[9] also, for example, to being silent and waiting. The latter is integrated into the term "action" because I understand it as an action of and between human beings

---

9   Cf. J. Habermas, *Zur Logik der Sozialwissenschaften* (Frankfurt/M. 3/1973) pp. 138-164.

where not only speaking and giving have a place, but also silence and receiving, not only activity but also suffering.

We have reached now a brief anthropological background to understand the following more clearly: especially how the Bible deals with the word "God".

2.2 *Biblical Stories of God*

If we consider the experiences with God in the Old Testament then in the very first revelation of the name Yahweh we see something unusual and at the same time characteristic. This name "I am who I am or who I will be" (cf. Ex 3,14) contains no general or abstract quality which could be used to name God (by, for example, superlatives such as "all-bountiful", "omnipotent" or "omniscient"). The name says "only" that God is and will be there. It describes in this form a personal existence which cannot be obviously determined on a level which is detached from the concrete and real experience. In this respect the name is "empty" or rather it is open for a meaning which still has to be experienced. This is concurrent with the Old Testament commandment that one should not make for oneself a graven image of God (cf. Ex 20,4; Dtr 5,8).

In the Bible the name of God only achieves meaning because it is told and discovered in connection with very specific encounters and experiences. The name "Yahweh", for example, becomes meaningful in connection with the remembrance of the Exodus story or with other experiences of God's people: God is known through these stories and experiences and moreover as someone who stands on the side of the people and does not withdraw his trust and frees them from sin and oppression. The name Yahweh in Israel is thus not determined by a summary of meaningless, abstract qualities and titles full of authority (although these also exist, they are always in the context of, or as a result of concrete experiences, in particular in the use of the psalms in prayer). God achieves moreover meaningful contours by the fact that he can be related with reference to real experiences in dynamic verbs, that is, in the dimensions of encounters and actions. (The verbal-structure of the Hebrew language is indeed the fitting linguistic medium for that purpose). Otherwise there is no longer a connection with the biblical God.

This process is always concerned with unique, very different stories which cannot be copied and which are very different, which, however, always "illustrate" the same in their differentiated situations and people: this very same is the liberating devotion of God in the history of mankind. The experience with God illuminates the fragments of human life like the light in a prism with very contrasting colours, which are due to the possibilities and impossibilities, the richness and limitation of real people. Of course, there is nothing to be said against theologians who with logic argumentatively and speculatively consider how one may reflect on God and what one may further say about him. This "systematic theology", however, should not lose its contact with its basis of stories and experiences, in which the decisive and unique interpersonal encounters take place between God and mankind which are thereby made possible for future experiences. Only a illustration of the term God through such memories redeems and releases us from having to produce God ourselves in our thoughts or to subordinate him to our argumentative or even magical access.

It is clear here that the biblical personality of God maintains the secret of God for, although one can name him in such unique stories of encounters, he does not become generally definable. The Old Testament, which is always accused of being too anthropomorphous and of referring too much to God in human terms, here displays itself as a critical stronghold against a theology which wants to ensnare God in thoughts and seize him by means of systematical connections. Inasmuch as this theology wants to possess something of God, it is more anthropomorphous than to tell of God in the context of concrete interpersonal stories because these stories remain open in their uniqueness of the you and I/we relationship for new stories in the present and the future in which God enters into new and unique encounters with new people. In this way his promise made in the memory of the old stories will be realized once again in a different way than it can be calculated and foreseen by us humans.

Already in the written word, differing, in part contradictory human stories of experiences of the same God come together, so that neither unity nor a freedom from contradiction are characteristic for the presence of God in such stories of which there are many, even contradictory ones because they all only come from individual people, however general they claim their thoughts to be. The answer to the justified question as to the "unity" of a definition of God cannot be given in a theological system of thought which requires the agreement of all believers, mostly in the form of church structural subordination (mystificated by the term "Hierarchy"). The unity exists rather in the fact that the different stories supplement each other as unique stories in their untouched individuality as well as in their ability and need for mutual interchange. This subject will be expanded further below in chapter eight.

Moreover, the stories of Yahweh contain a characteristic double structure which is discussed in theology in the determination of the relationship between the Indicative of God's mercy and the Imperative of human behaviour, between given talents and using these talents. God is experienced as a liberating and faithful companion and helper in one's own distress. He provokes a particular interpersonal relationship and allows and enables us to act in a just as helping and liberating way with other people. Both dimensions related to the presence of God in the history of the people are given in special stories; Israel remembers the Exodus story from the viewpoint of the liberation of God, Israel remembers individual stories of the prophets which never arbitrarily referred to the will of Yahweh but made perfectly clear that the belief in Yahweh, that his word is only compatible with a definite spiritual, social and political praxis. That these texts which thematisize human behaviour are quite different in character and exist in tension with each other, is apparent because of the differences between the people, situations and because of the different radicality or willingness to compromise. Here also we see the mutual ability and need for interchange so that throughout the history of many stories one may experience what it means to organize one's life and act according to the will of God.

2.3 *Jesus's Practical References to God*

The embodiment of God which began in the Old Testament achieves its deepest foundation and realization in Jesus of Nazareth. God becomes human through Jesus and takes the responsibility himself for his own practical "historical" and unique definition. The presence of God in history is then determined from that point onwards by the history and the remembrance of the story of Jesus Christ. God does not "come from on high" in the form of ruling knowledge to mankind and does not appear before mankind in a showy overbearing display, dispensing redemption as a decree: "Because I am love, you are all redeemed!". He rather risks himself to show that he is love; he himself risks a story in which he appears and in which he realizes himself in the words and deeds of a particular human being. He shows his love in the detail of a single man. In order to explain himself God points at his only beloved son, as it is told and illustrated in the story of the baptism of Jesus: "And when Jesus...was praying, the heaven was opened...and a voice came from heaven, `thou art my beloved son; with thee I am well pleased'" (Lk 3,21 ff.). God shows us the real human being Jesus: look at him, then you will know who has a relationship to God; then you will know what the kingdom of God means. Who God is and what mankind could and should be is given its meaning by the actions of this man and his relationship to God and mankind.

Let us now also consider the story of the transfiguration of Jesus on Mount Tabor. Here God also points to Jesus and refers to his words and actions: "That is my son, my chosen, listen to him!" (Lk 9,28-36, here 35). Those involved must once again descend to the ground level of mankind and the transfiguration has no value of its own but shows itself to be the "enthronement" of the human life of Jesus of Nazereth and his way to the cross, which he risked for the sake of love and as a result of the necessarily connected criticism of the inhumanity of those in power. To deal with God has to be a very earthly thing. Only as such it is heavenly enough.

Accordingly Jesus does not speak of God outside of concrete healing and participating actions, outside redeeming and saving encounters. In doing so, he stands in the tradition of the prophets of Israel who claimed that mankind behaves in the way God has behaved with

them, in that mankind works for justice to all
and for mercifulness towards everyone and does
not hide injustice and mercilessness by pious
words. He speaks of and demonstrates the kingdom of God when he carries out his mission of
mercy and salvation in encounters with the
poor, the stigmatized and the weak or when he
forgives in God's name those who have sinned.
He also speaks of the kingdom of God when in
his stories and parables he shows solidarity with
the poor and suffering. 'When I heal with my
finger on my hand, drive out terrible alienation
and speak and act against the marginalization of
the suffering and the excluded then the kingdom of God has reached you!' In his realized as
well as related stories, the term "God" is en-
dowed with an unmistakable practical unambiguity. These stories do not exclude the suffering
world but incorporate it and relate the effect of
God amongst the people in it. The effect of
God is such that it always concentrates itself on
the basic contradiction between those who
create suffering and those who fight against
suffering and risk themselves in this contradiction.

Jesus thus demonstrates (Lk 11,4-5) the
"truth" of his Gospel and his sending in answer
to John the Baptist in that he allows his healing
deeds to be related with reference to Isaiah:
"The blind receive their sight, the lame walk,

lepers are cleansed, the deaf hear...the poor have good news preached to them." The Lord will thus ask us if we have given the hungry food or if we have welcomed strangers and have visited the sick in his name (cf. Mt 25, 31-46). Strangely enough, the Lord will obviously not question what we have believed. The religious outsider in the Samaritan story is the justified one because he helped the suffering man and the priest who was hurrying to the temple to serve God in the so-called "real way" did not understand anything (cf. Lk 10, 25-37). And Peter's verbal acceptance of Christ and his flight from following the suffering Messiah also belong here: Peter is blessed for his profession of faith as the "rock" of the church and is called Satan for his flight from the real imitation of the surrendering and powerless Messiah.

These are the details by which the kingdom of God becomes reality in the history of mankind. The criteria are explicitly of a practical nature! The conflicts with those who, although they also talk of Yahweh, show counter-effective behaviour and conduct (namely, they cheat people of their rights and freedom) are predetermined. The deadly conflict explodes due to the irreconcilable contradictory deeds of the adversaries which they associate with the definition of God.

2.4 *Limited Plurality*

The plurality of different ways of praxis under the term "God" has its decisive limits at the point where disadvantaged, oppressed and suffering people are concerned *and* where one is only allowed to associate his praxis explicitly with the definition of God, if he solidarizes with these people. Jesus's treatment of the sinners and the message of God's forgiveness show that this praxis is not to be thought of in a perfectionistic and rigorous way. Whoever does not search for and attempt this way of humane praxis and is not willing to change his or her life accordingly has forfeited his right to claim the term "God" for his "stories". Whoever speaks of God from this point on will only then "prove him to be true" for the experience of others when he tries to act in the same way as Jesus Christ.

Jesus cures the linguistic problems of mankind with respect to the definition of God in the way that he extracts this term by means of his own story out of the "paradoxical communication" (as it is called by social-psychologists) in which the term God is linked to a praxis of the oppression and destruction of people which is contradictory to its authentic reality. That exactly has always been the pathological problem in church history: to connect evil deeds with the talking of a loving God. Whoever follows Jesus's speaking of God within the context of healing deeds does not only become involved in the recovery of the authentic definition of God, but at the same time in the realization of his presence in mankind.

Therefore the narrative structures of the Bible are so important, because its stories contain related praxis and provoke a new real and comparable praxis in the present. Thus the argument of words will become the argument of deeds and ways how to live. What the comparison between the related definition of "God's will" and the real conduct (of the people) then makes possible is the structure of action and communication inherent in both.

The theo-linguistic consequence is therefore that a term is not available and usable as a mere theory without having its real role-play, its dramaturgy. Otherwise it loses its meaning and contact with reality and becomes practically arbitrary. The application of terms for the unarbitrary in reality (and not in the sense: "anything goes"[10]) gives way to its unambiguous understanding and realization: then, as a matter of fact, God's word happens further in deed.

The freedom to interpret the stories of the Bible finds its limits in the past neediness which

---

10 See P. Feyerabend, *Irrwege der Vernunft* (Frankfurt/M. 1989), (Farewell to reason 1986).

has been narrated and in the neediness in the actual experience of need by both the suffering people themselves and all those who notice and sense them. Neediness (the English word for the German "Not-Wendigkeit", which implicates that need has to be twisted) is the hermeneutic circle, which they have in common: both, the stories of the past and the stories of the present, as stories of victims. Jesus's own story was the story of a victim. Such a convergence of horizons is a precondition for the authentic reception not only of the Bible but of the tradition as a whole. Diaconia shows itself to be the theoretical as well as realistic hermeneutic horizon of authentic encounters between believer and tradition.

On closer inspection this is not a limitation of freedom in dealing with the past but a defence against ambiguity which easily runs the danger of endangering the freedom of others. Whoever does not read biblical stories from the perspective of mercifulness and justice, will quickly use them ideologically as confirmation (of the existing social contradictions) and misuse them more. The horizon of diaconia, as it has already formed the best biblical stories, can be achieved only at the moment when this viewpoint is understood by the readers as a matter of concern and experience. In fact this process can be regarded as a kind of "materialistic hermeneutics" (at least as a counterpart to a mere spiritual or intellectual approach).

Exactly this process *is* the church in its real creative and spiritually stimulating quality, where the encounter with God is the place where redeeming and liberating actions and political solidarity are achieved and decided. For God is and desires the redemption of mankind and accompanies those who attempt to bring his redemption into the history of mankind. In this process it is not unusual for sacrifices to occur because the helping person who proclaims the human God himself encounters disadvantages and even life threatening situations. This happens as a parallel to Golgotha. And, on the other hand, those stories are stories of hope, going through Golgotha to reach the vitality of God, who raises the dead and blesses those who are apparently without hope with his promise of life.

The unity between word and deeds which fulfil the words as they occur, for example, in Jesus's stories of healing also qualify the inner structure of his *spoken* communication. Questions, problems or terms facing him are explained by him not by abstract syllogisms but with stories of examples and parables in which the meaning is made clear.[11] He thus tells in the

---

11 Cf. E. Arens, *Kommunikative Handlungen* (Düsseldorf 1982) pp. 325-337.

parable of the labourers in the vineyard the narrated dramaturgy of that which one should understand by the terms Heaven and its justice (cf. Mt 20,1-16). The "God-given" definition of these terms clearly contrasts sharply with the conventional terms of justice regulated by punishment or exchange or achievement as is usual in the praxis of our society and as could be demonstrated by many merciless stories of experience. In this way, Jesus does not only confront terms (whose abstract contradiction as already discussed can be easily weakened or even removed by clever rationalization), but sets related praxis against real praxis. Their difference can no longer be ignored or discussed away. In connection with this story the Christian preaching of justice can no longer only be an intellectual discourse on justice but has to make the narrated definition the basis for consideration and to seek out such stories and suggestions for action which correspond factually to the biblical model. In attempting to create a possibility for existence for the dimensions of the kingdom of God in this world and the present, one will endeavour to transfer these narrated structures of action into the often unwieldy and counter-effective actions of mankind.

3. The Messiah as a Diaconical Figure

3.1 *Sensibility and Solidarity*

What do the actions of Jesus of Nazereth, the praxis which the Messiah himself combines with the term and will of God, look like on closer examination? How does he treat the poor, how does he behave diaconically and how does he treat the suffering? How do the disadvantaged become not only receivers of his help and liberation but also people who have important things to say and who, in turn, represent help and rewarding experiences for the lives of the helpers? I would like to present several examples which appear to me as being decisive in our topic as a whole.

– Jesus deals with people in a "physical" and gentle way.

Despite some of the formal reductions in the existent texts by corresponding literary schemes, many of the stories of encounters with Jesus in the Gospels have still retained their original character of unavoided corporeality. Jesus allows the leper to approach him and touches him (cf. Mt 8,3) and allows the woman who had suffered a haemorrhage to touch him (cf. Mt 9,20). Jesus does not hesitate also to mix his spittle with the earth to rub into the eyes of the blind man (cf. Jn 9,6). It is also a part of this manifestation of human contact that Jesus allows time for conversation (cf. Mt 15,21-28) and that he often reacts and acts in the most sensitive and appropriate way towards the people and situations. In this feature, I think for example of the encounter with the adulterous woman (cf. Jn 8,3-11). Jesus does not accuse her, rather he downgrades the self-appointed judges and their moral laws, which are, literally, written in *stone* and can easily be used as stones. Silently *he* writes in the *sand* of the earth and thus rescues the situation and the "sinner". No person deserves physical punishment because of actual or alleged infringement of moral principles! The fact that Jesus reacts in this way to the situation is one aspect in his way of treating people in person.

When one considers that here literary re-workings of real encounters of Jesus are concerned, then one can hardly imagine the warmth of feeling and trust, the communicative and therapeutic power and the physical dimension in his encounters intensively enough! The overcoming of the fear of contact with ill people, outsiders and lepers is the helping and merciful power of the Holy Spirit in the saints of past and present days, who root the security of their lives in God and as a result of such belief (like Francis of Assisi) kiss and embrace the lepers.

3.2 *Jesus Heals and Forgives*

Jesus realized the existence of physical and mental need around him and, in liberating encounters, healed the sick, drove out demons and forgave sins. The fact that Jesus appeared as a worker of miracles is amazing but not unusual for his contemporary socio-cultural environment. Jesus thus practices a "conventional" form of healing for that time. He confronts the experiences of pain and reacts to them in the most effective way possible. According to A. Suhl the miracles are "a definite protest against real human suffering, against the suffering of the ill, the maimed and the isolated".[12] The stories of miracles are therefore not (only) there to support the belief in the authority of God in Jesus (such belief should be based after all in the

---

12 A. Suhl (ed.), *Der Wunderbegriff im Neuen Testament* (Darmstadt 1980) pp. 1-38 (Introduction), p. 38.

message of the resurrection), rather they refer to his praxis of realizing the existence of need, of wanting to communicate with the suffering and to help them as much as possible and to show solidarity with them.

The sobering and principally diaconical basic structure of the stories of healing may not be disregarded in favour of the mounting stylization of the term "miracle", which is already present in the New Testament, or in favour of the ever popular and even new modern tendency to debate on this term! The miracles are not the "be all and end all" of Christian belief! They are not really important, because if you believe only in Christ's miracles, then you easily forget the purpose they have, the purpose of diaconia. The miracles have no meaning for their own sake, quite against the anthropology of general religions concerning the miracles as the religious belief's dearest child.

The healing of Jesus is not only closely linked in meaning with the message of redemption, but his message of redemption is in turn closely linked in its material effect with healing! If one cannot refrain from referring to the miracles, then one must see the miracles in their strict functional context of diaconia; God confirms in the miracle of healing the fact that Jesus may go beyond the existing natural or legal norms for the sake of suffering people. The miracles are thus a "judgement of God" for the radical diaconia of Jesus at any time and in any place against anything which could prevent and obstruct this diaconical action.[13]

The motivation for this helping and liberating behaviour of Jesus is his compassion and often emotively described mercifulness (the need of mankind moves and shocks him; cf. Mt 9,36; Mk 1,41; 6,34). "Primarily the poor and the sick learn what it means that they are more important for Jesus – and for God, as Jesus tells us – than even the Sabbath, the law. Mercifulness thinks and acts according to the suffering people".[14] The miracles make clear the prevalence of diaconical behaviour. "Only the realization that God places himself through the miracles on the side of action which breaks through the norms, removes the uncertainty and leads to the praise of God (Mk 2,12)".[15]

Jesus brings the suffering person into the innermost centre for this reason and makes him into the interrelative centre of his words and deeds. In this way Jesus takes the man with the withered hand (cf Mk 2,27-3,6) from the peri-

---

13 Cf. M. Dibelius, *Die Formgeschichte des Evangeliums* (Tübingen 6/1971) p. 144.

14 H. Seibert, *Diakonie – Hilfehandeln Jesu* (Gütersloh 1983) p. 35.

15 G. Theissen, *Urchristliche Wundergeschichten* (Gütersloh 1974) p. 118.

phery and places him in the centre, in this case in the centre of the synagogue. That is outstanding, because the centre is the place where the Thora, the word of God and God himself has his place. We are not concerned here with a mere centre of locality, but a theologically determined centre. Also worthy of mention here, alongside the aforementioned stories are his encounters with lepers, tax collectors, prostitutes and sinners. Many parables also belong here. The groups of poor people of that time receive their place in the centre because of their need for help (not because of any other precondition than that of hopeful expectation) and because of the fact that Jesus comes into such encounters with them. All this shows that the encounter with those needing help and with the weak belongs in the centre of every Christian communication and also in the Christian social form. In the moment of encounter with a person in need of help, nothing else is more important than this person, who needs recognition, an enhancement of status and support without regard to his or her culture, race, religion or denomination. His or her life is eternally valuable in the eyes of Jesus and his God. Christians, as the followers of Jesus of Nazereth, have to learn this eternal value of the suffering in their own way of life.

Exactly such moments of encounter with the disadvantaged are the special place where

Jesus teaches and where he speaks of the loving God and the message of the kingdom of God. The kingdom of God is here not a utopian ideality without a place in which one must believe and in which one can only believe, but is already, at least in part, a real manifestation which one can see! The credibility of Jesus lies only in part in his words about the kingdom of God and about God himself. His main credibility lies in his diaconical experiences with God and in his diaconical acts for the people. To put it the other way round; Jesus interprets with his message, in effect, "only" that which he does![16] The diaconical experience has thereby a central character of conveying the message, inasmuch as it partly makes possible the real experience of the kingdom of God which has become credible exactly because of it. The great importance of such an action in the message and the life of Jesus is shown in his call to follow him in a realistic way. That is possible to see in the story of the two brothers (cf. Mt 21,28-32), where the one son says no to his father's request to go to the vineyard, but in the end acts positively, whereas the other son who says yes does nothing. The first son is shown to be right by means of his deeds.

16 Cf. R. Zerfaß, Predigt im Prozeß der Gemeinde. In: id. (ed.), *Mit der Gemeinde predigen* (Gütersloh 1982) pp. 30–49, p. 36.

3.3 *Jesus Expects Decisive Messages from Those in Need*

When Jesus encounters suffering or "stigmatized" people, as well as those characterized in any way by loss and disadvantage[17] as well as by guilt, he places them in the centre of the current communication (cf. Mk 2,27-3,6). Jesus places the child in the centre who, then as now, is not an "equal" person because a child is not capable of taking a full part in official worship (or today does not belong to the achievement-orientated society) and is thus not yet an adult. He does this also against the attempts of his disciples to turn the children away because they did not consider them important enough for meeting him. At the same time more happens; the children and the fact of their childhood are displayed as an orientation of meaning for the adults and for the disciples who do not take the children seriously. They are made a measure against which a person has to learn how to deal with the kingdom of God. The child is thus not placed in the centre to be an object of helping actions, but becomes itself a personal criterion for how the so-called adults should behave

---

17 According to E. Goffman's definition, cf. id., *Stigma* (Frankfurt/M.) 1976, pp. 9-30.

towards life, mankind and God (cf. Mt 19,13-14; Mk 9,36). Jesus thus says: "Truly, I say to you, whoever does not receive the kingdom of God like a child shall not enter it" (Mk 10,15).

The healing of the blind man (cf. Mk 10,50) also shows that those affected have something to say. For Jesus does not heal him without being asked, but expressly asks "What do you want me to do for you?"

Jesus turns the tables: You can learn particularly from the young and from the weak how one deals with God and mankind. The weak but not the strong are the meaning-giving principle for the following of Jesus. This applies in two aspects. The strong (in this case the adults) open their perspective and put the young and weak in the centre. And they allow the formation of their community with one another and with God to be determined by these weak people. It is then clear that justice in a real context can only be determined and defined by those who have been deprived of justice. They have the competence to do it.

This moment of Jesus's communication with the suffering (in which they are credited with a particular meaningful competence) is revealed in an amazing way which has been almost ignored to date, in his healing encounters with the so-called possessed. The latter know who Jesus is, that he is the Son of God (cf. Lk 4,41). The "possessed" have something true to say.[18]

The suffering are therefore not only the target group of Jesus's liberating action, as he treats their problems, but they are accepted as important individuals exactly because of their suffering and they have something decisive to say. Therefore in diaconia, martyria (preaching) of a particular type takes place. As when one meets the son of mankind in the suffering, then one may be all the more certain that they are not only the target group of the diaconia but are and become also a creative group of the martyria in the church.

3.4 Jesus Supports the Suffering in Public

It is well known that Jesus did not only come into small groups but, on many occasions, was not afraid to make use of "mass communication" and openly and pointedly made his position clear. The argumentative discussions with the religious leaders of that time also belong to the public and political side of his actions. There are also very few parables in which,

18 Cf. O. Fuchs, Theologische Aspekte zur Interaktion mit psychiatrischen Patienten. In: *Wege zum Menschen 40* (1988) 2, pp. 87-95.

along with the individual encounters, a structural political perspective is not apparent in the choice of those involved. A classic example for this behaviour is contained in the parable of the Good Samaritan. In the answer to the question of the Pharasee "Who is my neighbour?", there follows the definition of this term not in an abstract way but pragmatically, that is, within the course of the action, but in two directions; on the one hand, in the direction of the narrower, interpersonal social area (that means the helping deed), on the other, in the direction of a sharp social criticism of the existing prejudices, since it is the Samaritan who helps after all (cf. Lk 17,11-19).

In this, as in many other stories, the structural aspect of sin is also involved and thematized. The prototype of those who belong to the negative group in the actual context is connected in the story with positive actions. The religious outsider is the one who helps the other, who is for him a stranger and an outsider. The story is thus also directed against the collective downgrading of the people concerned. The Samaritan is not on the level of the recounted story, but is however, on the level of the story between the narrating Jesus and his listeners, most certainly the victim; Jesus opposes his "status as a victim" by making him a model in the story and thereby attacking the ethno-centristic stereotypes which debase those who do not belong to one's own people.

The biblical stories are not divisible between the collective and the individual. They unfold their meaningful energy for the relationships between people as well as for those between social systems, groups, societies and nations. One must remember the stories of the prophets, whose socio-critical involvement in the context of their belief in Yahweh (as the helper of widows and the poor) is constitutive for their message. The aspect concerning structural sin between peoples becomes clear in Issiah 7,1-9 where King Ahaz has to decide between a military alliance or renouncing it, by means of trusting in God.

In the authentic following of the Old Testament socio-critical prophecy, Jesus lists the decisive social contradictions by name in his public speeches (cf. in particular the sermon on the mountain in Lk 6,20-49) and exposes them: "Blessed are you poor...but woe to you that are rich!" An individualization or therapization of diaconia cannot be justified. Political diaconia forms moreover an integral part of Jesus's redeeming treatment of the sick and the oppressed. The analysis of social, political and institutional reality has to be seen as an essential moment of his preaching itself. Belonging to diaconia are not only the immediate giving of help and the reduction or removal of suffering, but at the same time the search for the political conditions and structural origins which create suffering and the resulting socio-political and economic position. This has to be seen as an integral part of the term "diaconia".

– In diaconia, Jesus risks himself becoming an outsider

Jesus's relationship with the sick, the poor and the guilty along with his public support for these groups provokes the accusation of being possessed himself. His contemporaries judge his actions to be pure folly (cf. Lk 11,14ff.). His non-conformism and dissidence for the sake of diaconia appear to be signs of dangerous madness for those in power and eventually lead to his crucifixion. Whoever treats the suffering and oppressed with radical help and redemption attracts the anger of those who possess power at the expense of the disadvantaged. Jesus does not give up his struggle for mankind however, right up to the end. Precisely the "rich" are for him the real "fools" because they cling to deceptive and inhumane security and strategies which have no future in the kingdom of God (cf. Lk 12,20).

3.5 Jesus's Relationship to the Diaconia of God

One wonders where Jesus obtained the power
to consistently lead such a life right to the end.
The answer to this question leads us to his relationship with God which means here that he
believes in the God of Israel and finds himself in
the tradition of the communication of the
people with Yahweh. Thus he prays with the
words of the psalms and prophetic texts, he
knows the old stories of God's helping and redeeming treatment of his people. Jesus experiences the relation to God in a way which is
incomparable in its intensity. He finds his own
word for this, namely "Abba", the child's word
for a good and loving father. This is why he
seeks refuge for weeks on end in the desert.
This is why he tells of the love and justice of
God in parables. This is why he believes in the
coming kingdom of God. This is why he
laments at the end, in a situation of extreme
physical and spiritual need with the words of
Psalm 22 (cf. Mc 15,34).[19]

These are only indications of how much his
relationship with God formed the centre of his
existence, how much time he invested in this
relationship and how vital his encounters in

---

19 Cf. O. Fuchs, *Die Klage als Gebet. Eine theologische
Besinnung am Beispiel des Psalms 22* (München 1982).

prayers in the form of an I/you dialogue were. God is not a mere word for humanity but is himself a real helping and liberating partner in this life and beyond, who cannot be preached and represented in the history of mankind in any other way than as the advocate of human beings who need help and liberation. For Jesus, God and his kingdom do not only become concrete praxis in interhuman deed, but also in the relationship with God himself which can be experienced as reality through belief and which underlies the human relationship with other people in a facilitating way (see in detail chapter 4.4-5).

4. Christian Belief within Saving and Redeeming Experience

4.1 *The Benefitting Church*

I would like to start with a particular text which may serve as a preamble. The text is from Pope John XXIII who spoke these words a few days before his death. I understand these words as his legacy in the context of our subject: "In the presence of my colleagues, I am spontaneously moved to renew the act of belief. This is a proper thing for us priests, as we have to deal with the highest of matters for the good of the whole world and therefore we must allow ourselves to be led by the will of God. We are orientated more than ever today, certainly more than in the last centuries, to serve mankind as such and not only the Catholics and are orientated in the first instance and above all to defend the rights of mankind and not only those of the Catholic church. The present situation, the challenge of the last fifty years and a deeper understanding of belief have confronted us with a new reality, as I said in my speech opening the Council. It is not the Gospel which has changed; no, we are the ones who are just beginning to understand it better. When one has had a long life and has seen oneself confronted with the new tasks of a social engagement at the start of this century and when one has spent twenty years in the Orient and eight in France as I have done and as a result is able to compare different cultures, then one knows that the moment has come where we must recognize the signs of the times, where we must seize the possibilities offered and look to the future."[20]

I would like to underline the following sections of this text as I repeat them in the following summary: The act of belief, its renewal and dealing with the highest of matters have as their aim the well-being of the whole world. Therefore we are orientated today to serve mankind as such and not only the Catholics and are orientated in the first instance and above all to defend the rights of mankind and not only those of the Catholic church. In my opinion, these comments express in a highly concentrated form the basic intention of the II. Vatican Council.

Thus the issue is not only to "win" people for the church, but it is also the question as to what the church does with those people that it

20 Cf. *Orientierung No. 52,10* (1988) p. 109.

has already "won" for itself. Does it want to bring them into a ghetto-like (exculturated) church which only carries out the salvation of its own institution or does the church want to enable the people to humanize their environments because they are supported by a church which realizes itself for a more humane world and thereby for the kingdom of God (with all the fragmented quality and partiality of these attempts by Christians and the church to create as much reality as possible for the kingdom of God)? The knowledge of the Good News is therefore not to be spread in a privileged know-all manner or as a ruling knowledge, but as a knowledge in our faith which should be for the benefit, not only of ourselves, but also of as many people and cultures as possible. Thus it is not primarily a question of acquiring competence and authority for the most effective application of strategies, it is rather a question of for what purpose both are to be employed.

One can, for example, read and teach the biblical text in a competent way, from the perspective of knowledge and method, but still basically misunderstand the critical background of evangelizing, if one does not read the text principally and practically from the perspective of mercifulness and at least longed-for justice. When one does not approach biblical texts from the perspective of such practical hermeneutics for the benefit of mankind and particularly the suffering, then one will all too easily functionalize them for that which one wants to achieve (in particular for the benefit of a strong church). It is my concern therefore that we reach the basis of our identity and ask why we, as Christians and as the church, are there and are called to be such in the world.

In the theology of the II. Vatican Council a theological basis is given which can no longer be circumvented, to disarm dispensing with much which in the long term has a destructive effect for us and for others and to look what is possible for us and what is necessary for us according to the Gospel. Then, however, we must tackle that and act. Nothing should be understood in terms of "doing still more" and progressive excessive demands, which rightly provoke the reaction; we've got to do all that as well! It is more probable that we should not do some of the activities which are at present taking place and should devote this energy to those places which are more necessary according to the Gospel and those affected. It is possible to do less but to do that then with more courage to stand up for one's beliefs and courage to take up our position and to show solidarity with those who need mercifulness and justice.

The II. Vatican Council places the authentic unity of belief and life, dogma and pastoral,

teaching and praxis in the centre of its statements. It is here that we see in effect the dogmatic progress of this Council[21] (as without this
the encyclica "Evangelii nuntiandi" cannot be
sufficiently understood). In the present strategy
of forgetting and removing the importance of
the Second Council, it is repeatedly said that the
council has not announced any new dogma on
the semantic level, that is in the area of words,
and for this reason it is not so binding. Such a
conclusion is misleading. Of course, it is simply
not correct, because the dogmatic progress of the
Second Vatican Council, which is decisive for all
church dogmas, lies in the fact that the dimension of experience and praxis of the church's
teaching and thus of all its dogmas is questioned.
(Of course, the Council's texts should be read in
its deeper dimension and not just on the surface
where, in its formulation for the sake of compromise and achieving working majorities, it
can be used and quoted for completely differing
positions). We have many dogmas for which
the corresponding confessional agreement is demanded. At the same time, there is an
enormous deficit as regards their existential
meaning, concerning the people's daily life, that
is, their relevance to human existence. Which

---

21 Cf. E. Klinger, Der Glaube des Konzils. Ein dogma-
tischer Fortschritt. In: id./K. Wittstadt (ed.), *Glaube
im Prozeß* (Freiburg 1984) pp. 615-626.

experience and design of human life do the church's teachings challenge, offer and develop? Behind this is the unspoken idea that the treasures of our belief have been too little discovered to date for the communicative praxis of mankind and for the formation of social structures.

4.2 *The Practical Meaning of the Teaching*

This basic intention begins already with extreme consistency in the Dogmatic Constitution on Liturgy. In it the teaching of the sacrament as far as the Holy Mass is concerned and what the latter has to do with the teaching of the church in the context of apologetic and/or catechetical inculcations, is not only renewed and impressed upon us, but the universal question is as to how the Holy Mass must be organized and conducted so that the believers may experience what the church means by it in its teaching. The question of experience changes the liturgical praxis to date. In such a way the text is aware of the "signs of the time" which themselves have a theological quality. For this reason there is the extension of the service in word, the stress of the simplicity of symbols and above all the introduction of the vernacular.

This basic intention of the question as to how that which has been collected and "secured" in the teaching of the church for a long time finally develops its practical meaning for the people, is inherent in all the texts of the Vatican Council, above all the Dogmatic Constitutions "*Lumen gentium*" and "*Gaudium et spes*". The question which dominates the latter text is: If it is true what the church claims of itself in its teaching, namely that it is there for the salvation of the world and may be termed at least in an analogous sense as "sacramentum mundi", how must the church organize itself and be amenable for the world? Further, how must it deal with the world so that it can be really experienced as that what it claims to be, namely as salvation and redemption for the world in terms of the biblical message of God. In fact, quite a few systematic theologians have worked out that the Pastoral Constitution has to be regarded as the key-text in order to understand the II. Vatican Council as a whole. For in this text the church assesses itself from the outside perspective of itself. The meaning of the church is the response it elicits.

In the Constitution on the Church the same question is posed "towards the inside": How must the church develop itself so that its own members experience their existence in the church as a redeeming enrichment of their lives? For this reason you find the basic importance of placing the people of God before the hierarchy and the basic importance of the charismata of all (cf. Lumen Gentium No. 12).

Even the very heart of the matter, the Dogmatic Constitution on the Revelation, links the Revelation of God strictly with the experience of the biblical authors. Without their vocations in their characteristic qualities as well as in their one-sidedness and in their own particular historical situation, the revelation would not have been possible.[22] Here the term revelation is linked with ecclesiology: the substance of belief and the calling of people, which is practically experienced, belong together in the revelation *and* in the church. Revelation and the content of the teaching can never attain historical meaning and reality through mankind without the influence of mankind upon them. Reality can only be obtained in the unbreakable connection with human experience and lives, as well as with their diversity amongst each other which can even go so far as being contradictory. The biblical revelation shows, in correspondence to it, not only a *variety* of vivid events but not seldom different stories, which are *contrary* to each other. For example: You can hardly compare the fashion of belief (or better "non-belief"?) of Qoheleth (Ecclesiastes)

---

22 Cf. Dogmatic Constitution on the Divine Revelation No. 11.

68

with such a highly developed faith as you find with Deuteroisaiah. The same happens between the first letters of St.Paul and the so-called Pastoral letters concerning the church-structures. The lack of contradiction is none of the God's names neither in the revelation (which was once real life) nor in real life.

This is the exciting, revolutionary aspect of the II. Vatican Council: namely, that in its texts, which are called the "Dogmatic Constitutions", the question of praxis is approached. Thus, at the latest since the Council, pastoral theology can no longer be interpreted, due to strict theological reasons, as an applied science of dogmatics or of fundamental theology. Praxis belongs moreover to the dogmatic teaching of the church itself. The question as to the praxis of the church and Christians is not an application of dogma but is an integral part of it. This is precisely the dogmatic progress of the II. Vatican Council.

And here is also where the nail is hit squarely on the head; bringing up a painful subject for our church and for being a Christian! This is what educational theory calls "paradoxical communication", which is manifested, for example, in the combination of noble words with in part extremely despicable deeds. For many people the credibilty of the self-realization of the church is determined by the question: What is the praxis of the church like in the church itself and in its environment in comparison with its message of the redeeming and loving God? Where the meaningful connection of this talk of God is at odds with the praxis claimed by it, then the church reveals itself to be hardly attractive as a social offer of the Good News which would be its authentic identity.

We arrive at a further basic intention of the II. Vatican Council without which the term "evangelizing" in Catholic understanding cannot be understood and which also is connected in essence with the aforementioned intention. If the question as to the human praxis and ability to be experienced is itself a part of the dogma, then the question as to each individual believer and his or her meaning for the church now becomes vitally important. For this reason the Pastoral Constitution concerns itself extensively with the *calling of Christians*.

Thus the relationship between word and deed is linked with a very specific theology of calling of Christians. The texts of the II. Vatican Council give prominence to the calling of people in an amazing way. The Pastoral Constitution takes up its whole first section with this subject (section 1-57). It thus agrees with the People-of-God-Theology of the Church Constitution. "Belief illuminates everything in a new light, it reveals the divine decision with regard to the integral calling of mankind and orientates the spirit towards really humane solutions" (Gaudium et Spes No. 11). The council thus made "the calling of the people to the focal point of faith".[23]

The dispensation of baptism is not only the fulfillment of the church's obligation to spread the Good News (through word and sacrament), but it is simultaneously the advance payment for the duty corresponding to a Christian life and social behaviour; not only as the duty of the individual Christian to make something for mankind and society out of his calling in the following of Jesus, but also as a duty for the church and its representatives to believe in the calling of the baptized. The gift in the sacrament and the evoked duty return at the same time as the social responsibility to the person responsible for the preaching of this sacrament. This responsibility is to realize this reality, which is presented in the sacrament, in their communicative behaviour to the receivers of baptism. That which the church preaches and spreads as a gift of mercy does not only have consequences for the lives of those receiving it, but for those conveying it and for the social organization of the church.

---

23 Cf. E. Klinger, Der Glaube an den Menschen – eine dogmatische Aufgabe. In: *Theologie und Glaube 78* (1985) pp. 229 – 238, p. 230.

Those are thus both of the basic orientations of the council texts: namely, firstly, the unity of belief and life on the basis of the second aspect, the importance and responsibility of all those baptised and confirmed. The latter (and here I can only be brief) happens principally through the demonopolizing of the term "vocation", which, up to now, has been mainly reserved for clerics and members of religious orders, but which is now expanded for the whole of God's people. I emphasize this important double structure of the basic intentions of the Council for the reason that this hermeneutic key function for all texts is mostly not sufficiently acknowledged. It is my opinion that the great "miracle" of the II. Vatican Council lies in the fact that the self-deprivation of power is being carried out in the centre of power of the institution itself and that the responsibility for the formation of the church is being shared through communal responsibility and the involvement of all.

With such a "fundamental democratization" of the church based on a new theology of vocation, the Council again raises another painful subject which is of decisive meaning for diaconia; namely, the fact that there are many people who are wounded by and frightened of the church for the precise reason that inside the church the importance of the individual for the establishment of social structures of the church, as well as the responsibility of the individual for the belief of the church (in particular in differences of opinion and in cases of conflict) is too seldom accepted and called for (for more details see below chapter 8). I remind here of the fitting sentence, which Paul VI. wrote a decade later in his encyclica "Evangelii nuntiandi", that the different callings of the believers "make up the richness and beauty of the evangelization" (that is, of the church – O.F.).

4.3 *The Unarbitrary Nature of Praxis*

I would like to make clear what the praxis- and person-orientated theology of the II.Vatican Council stands for by means of a brief example concerning the sacrament of confirmation. This example has the advantage that both intentions explain and need each other. For the connecting and unifying of practical *experience* with the *teaching* of the confirmation is at the same time identical with the importance of taking the *charismata* seriously for the formation of the church. The sacrament of confirmation is as a rule administered in the context of an impressive liturgical scenario. The young people are told with great insistence, already in the preparation as well as in the administering liturgical service of the sacrament, that they have the Spirit of God and that they should believe that they are carriers of this Spirit. The problem is, however, that many administers and quite a number of priests, although they themselves believe *in* the confirmation (as far as what the *teaching* says about the sacrament of confirmation), have massive difficulties with the praxis which is necessarily connected with it: namely, when it comes to the practical test, to believe their word, when it is really necessary to trust in and to the confirmed young people and to deal with them according to the positive prejudice which the confirmation theologically intends for them, that means to expect from the people important statements, which are possibly enriching and indispensable for the building up of the community.

To believe "in confirmation" is one thing, it is another to introduce the potential value of life (which the confirmation contains) into the real communication of the church and, on this basis of the importance of all charismata, to organize the social forms of the church.

It belongs to the appropriate recognition of the II. Vatican Council, not only to encourage the people to accept and believe the teachings of the church, but above all, to always question and look for what is really the meaning of a certain teaching as far as the experience, the praxis and the pastoral aspects are concerned. In the example of the confirmation it is relatively clear that we have to make up for lost time with regard to the practical value of the believed dogmata. Great demands of belief are often made by those who do not realize the praxis which should be connected with their demands. Is it possible here that Jesus's word that one should observe and practise what the ministers tell you, but not what they do (cf. Mk 23,3 and Lk 11,46) applies to the officials of the church? This criticism is, of course, true for all Christians. I am convinced that the more we Christians concern ourselves with the praxis of that which we believe, the less we will have to worry about the continued existence of the church and the less we will have to reckon with approval from the false side (that is, from directions which think that they could use the Christian view of the world for a praxis which is contrary to the kingdom of God).

The theology of Jesus, or rather his theopraxy, is directed towards a mentality within the church in which the question of praxis is dealt with a good deal more arbitrarily and in a more egalitarian way than the unambiguity of faith in the field of the correct profession of belief. If, for example, a catechetic teacher has openly admitted problems with the dogma of the resurrection, then he will not easily be spared difficulties relating to his employment. If, however, he deals with the pupils for years on end in a despising way, then as a rule he has no problems as far as his employment is concerned. Characteristically, the term "heresy" is more established on the level of the consensus of belief than it touches the praxis which is connected with belief (to avoid misunderstanding here, I do not wish to introduce the term "heresy" also on the level of praxis, but only to make the reduction of the term "faith" significant with this example).[24]

4.4 *The Diaconical Dimension of Believing and Preaching*

There is not only an unarbitrary relationship between faith and its social praxis within our daily lives, but also within the faith itself, between belief and its spiritual praxis, between the word of God and its liberating experience within our existence. Speaking of the diaconical dimension of the Church we may not forget the diaconical dimension of the Christian message of God itself. Preaching God's presence in

---

24 Cf. H. Dietzfelbinger, Diakonie als Dimension der Kirche. In: H.-H. Ulrich (ed.), *Diakonie in den Spannungsfeldern der Gegenwart* (Stuttgart 1978) pp. 112–118.

the word and in the world is a part of this theme, because talking of diaconia one must not only think of the interhuman relationship of justice and help. It is rather an integral part of the diaconia-subject that the first deacon in Christian life is God himself, his love and help for mankind. To speak of this love of God towards us ourselves has to be regarded as one of the most important tasks of Christian preaching which wants to convey God's unconditional acceptance to the people: towards an indicative and facilitating speaking of God in the church.[25]

This subject has also biographical roots within my own life. In the first years of being minister in a parish I always strove (like my contemporary colleagues) to change the world, especially the Christians, to become more effective in their actions for freedom and justice, their actions for the sake of others. I interpreted the biblical stories mostly as ethical imperatives. Until I realized by means of the criticism of the people and of talks with my colleagues, that such a preaching is only half of what we have to say; yes, such a continual imperative preaching robs the believers of the facilitating possibility to love and help one another, which is the redeeming relationship with God himself.

---

25 Cf. in detail O. Fuchs, *Von Gott predigen* (Gütersloh 1984).

Forgetting is one of the worst things (especially according to the Old Testament[26]) which can happen to a community or a person, when matters are concerned which are vital for life and which stay alive merely by means of memory. When a subject is not constantly discussed and is made current in togetherness (and if it is not being related to a direct reality) then it gives way to the creeping loss of relevance and becomes marginal.

The sermon is a decisive institution within the Christian and ecclesiastical community of remembrance, to act against such forgetfulness in its constant work of remembering and thereby maintaining the memoria. As regards the contents of their memories, Christians rely on the stories from the Bible, in particular the story of Jesus Christ. The biblical stories substantialize for them a characteristic relationship, which is manifested in constantly new occasions of experience: the relationship of God with the people and the people's relationship to God. In this "theological horizon", encounters within mankind also take place, become important there and become possible and necessary in their humanity.

---

26 Cf. C. Westermann, *Lob und Klage in den Psalmen* (Göttingen 1977) p. 192.

This formulation of a "theological horizon" is obviously very approximate and open and requires a more precise definition, in particular the most essential: this divine area of humanity has itself the structure of encounter, of a realistic relationship which is often explicitly enough discussed and remembered, for example, in the stories of vocation, in the texts of prayer and particularly in Jesus's relationship to God (see above chapter 3.5). The related dialogues between God and people have a character of interaction where both partners make use of the word (in calling or prayer) whereby they are completing "speech-acts"[27] and whereby they initiate actions. Yahweh, the God of Israel and Abba, the God of Jesus is a God who wants, creates and maintains relationships.

That is the theological horizon where the relationships within mankind have their place, their value and are facilitated. It would not be a good theology to talk here of the horizontal and vertical dimension of biblical interpersonal reality or spirituality. Both these areas of communication are (undivided and unmixed) "meshed" together, namely, in the fact that they explain each other, recognize and deepen each other and identify one another. When one

---

27 Cf. J.R. Searle, *Sprechakte. Ein sprachphilosophischer Essay* (Frankfurt/M 1971), (Speech Acts 1969).

speaks of God's redeeming encounters with mankind, one implicitly speaks of the encounter of the people amongst themselves, which becomes possible because of this given relationship with God. When one encounters people in a benevolent way, one realizes implicitly the structure of communication of God with mankind. The modality of the discourse is however different. When one speaks of God's encounter, one speaks mainly in the indicative; when one speaks of the relationship of people amongst themselves, in the horizon of this God, one speaks in the imperative so long as the kingdom of God has not fully arrived, so that its constantly new comparative advancement to the present is put forward.

The indicative of the relationship granted by God is something given and offered, whereby this "being given" already reveals itself in its *form* of conveyance, in the remembrance of the corresponding examples which are given in the biblical *stories*. For telling stories conveys narrated interactions and is therefore open for spontaneous identifications. If you listen to stories you do not need as much effort to understand them as if you had to listen to a lecture or even to a sermon (if it does not tell stories, parables, metaphors etc. itself).

Thereby these stories which are committed to memory are not only valid for the narrated

people within these stories themselves, but carry
– in the horizon of God's lasting love – the
promise within them, to be valid for ever, so
that the process of memory simultaneously proclaims its validity throughout history and makes
itself and God's grace behind it present. Of such
a kind is the biblical understanding of 'zkr' (the
Hebrew word which means "memoria" or
"remembrance") insofar as the stories become
true and real, become substantialized by means
of telling and believing them in a community.
Precisely this indicative should not be forgotten
in Christian preaching; the "givenness" of a
God who wants encounter with mankind and
encourages mankind to enter into communication with him (even beyond death and the end
of the world). Such a desire for encounter on
the part of God also has a slight imperative part:
God offers himself for encounter, but mankind
has also to involve itself, so that he succeeds.
This imperative is, however, the result of a
indicative which can be realized; as the offer of
a unbreakable friendship, which wants to make
friends, to allow friendship to be experienced!
The biblical literature of prayer and its richness
of the speech-act of praise and thanks, lament
and bidding clearly shows how central the lively
dialogue with God expresses and interprets
human life within such a relationship. There is
nothing in human life which should be exclud-

ed from this vital encounter with God and the "diaconia" he has shown to the people.

When Christian preaching takes the fact seriously that this process of interaction between God and mankind makes real encounters possible, then God cannot only be spoken of as a cypher, a word for more humane communication, but also so that the concrete human relationship with God becomes a subject itself and a reality on its own. If God were only an idea in the biblical tradition, an abstract, an absolute, a neutrum, an ideal, an idealistic and intellectual dimension, then one could quite rightly say: "God – that means that we are good to each other". But then the biblical God becomes forgotten in his concrete nature and personality, in his anthropomorphous partnership to mankind. Accordingly one should say; "God – that means that he is good to mankind and also shows this!" Only such an indicative makes the imperative possible and releases it from obeying the laws and mankind from the craze of achievement or despair and resignation.

4.5 *Against "God" as a Term of Achievement!*

It cannot go further in this way (especially in the so-called left-wing Christian preaching) to transfer too quickly the talk of God to the talk of mankind, for example in such sentences as "Mercy, that means that we have to treat each other with mercifulness!", "Resurrection means that we should not fall, but always get up again!" etc. In such sentences concerning God himself the connection with interaction is extinguished. But only this interpersonal connection makes up the point of reference and context in the framework of its validity and possibility. This point is; mercy means that God is merciful to you; with such an experience of belief behind one, a human being can also be "merciful". Resurrection means that God resurrects a person who has died for the love of mankind and for the sake of its liberation, and thereby continues his life further and also legitimizes it; with such an eschatological deed, it is also possible for a human being to risk a similar life "for no reward" against a lack of success and the suspicion of senselessness.

Where God is not constantly discussed in homiletic discourse, preached in sermons and addressed in prayers as the personal communication partner of the people, then their actions reduce themselves mercilessly to obeying laws of the exemplary. To present Jesus only as an example of benevolence is the personified lawmaking of the Christian message and thereby is a hopeless overtaxing of human beings, inasmuch as Jesus's God and his own relation to him, which has made such a life possible, are omitted.

The depersonalizing of God leads to the moralizing of mankind! "God" is supercharged with directions for actions which mankind has to do itself. May I remind in this context of Lk 11,46: "And Jesus said, 'Woe to you lawyers also! For you load men with burdens hard to bear!'" God is preached as a term of achievement and not as the communicative facilitator of the possibility for a more humane life and history. That is a distressing conforming to the structure of achievement of late capitalist and highly industrialized societies and their fantasies of total power, even to the attitude that God could be at our disposal by means of Ethics. That is a kind of atheism within Christianity. The belief in progress for a complete and saved world which is to be achieved by mankind provokes already in many places either violence or resignation.

Many modern sermons are not much different in their structure than the old casuistic and moralistic way of preaching, even though the purposes have changed. In both cases theological issues become too quickly directions for action; the interpretation of God is functionalized and fades to the religious-argumentative legitimation of what one has to say to mankind as the imperative. This is also true of attractive contemporary sermons even if their form of address does not display any *direct* commands or laws, but is characterized by dream-filled, aesthetic and poetic images and stories which, although they allow more freedom than direct demands, still interpret God as the area of action of the good people. Biblical theology, on the other hand, claims that the talk of God is not a mythical statement of purely human qualities, hopes and actions, but that the biblical myth presupposes the reality and reality of encounter of that which it talks about.

Such a "boomerang-preaching", which throws the vector of the human relationship to God back to the relationship of the people among themselves (prayer as a conversation with oneself) and with others (God as human benevolence), can only be based on sporadically used sections of the Bible with the help of short-sighted and naive hermeneutics. This is true for example of the story of the two sons, where one of them says "yes", but does not go to the vineyard and the other says "no", but goes to work there after all. The story annuls in its message not the relationship orientated "yes" to the Lord, but has as its aim to not let this "yes" stand on its own, but to fill it with the corresponding practical and humane meaning (cf. Mt 21,28-32).

The difficult and precarious question about God cannot be answered by simply creating identities: "God is identical with benevolence",

"The confession to Jesus Christ is basically identical with living as Jesus lived as far as our fellow human beings are concerned". Such identifications do not solve the "problem" between mankind and God, they destroy it. Simultaneously such an identity of mankind with God destroys God as a real encountering partner.

In opposition to many trends of individual moralizing (with regard to marriage and the family) as well as socio-political moralizing of the biblical horizon of God, we should try to realize God as an independent reality of partnership and thus to respect him as the meaningful place of relationship from which such activities for the sake of mankind and its society become possible even over long distances in distress (and at the same time are to be criticized by the liberating character of God's deeds). Thus, the Christians can involve themselves to the point of courage of sacrifice for peace in the different areas of life and between peoples and show solidarity with the appropriate movements. At the same time, with their belief in God, they bring the necessary condition to have patience and stamina for long distances and also in planning stages as well as to bring up the corresponding theological criticism of human activities.

How then should preachers speak? That this is homiletic "hard work" is already known by preachers who endeavour to verbalize the theological indicative of our faith, in so far as a sermon can do it. My plea for the indicative "talk of God" should not be euphorically or charismatically misunderstood, as if one could overcome the problem when one speaks pathetically and conjures up the reality of God by asking for special experiences of vocation against which most listeners would be helpless. The sermon which is meant here should not transfer the work itself has to do to the listeners; the sermon has to do the work of remembrance itself with the help of the biblical texts, with whose narrative and spiritual (especially concerning the psalms) hermeneutic power similar encounters of God can be made possible, as they are found in the stories. On the other hand the sermon should do this work listening to the listeners, to the baptized believers and their experiences of God (which include the lack of such experiences, too) and correlating them in an encouraging way with the biblical events. Doing this the sermon would be the bridge between the inspiring stories of the inspired Bible and the inspiring experiences of the inspired Christians. Talking of God thus provokes an extremely sober and realistic work of preaching, which is concerned with the experiences, situations and memories of the people, both of the past (in the tradition) and of the present (in the church).

5. The Church as Evangelization

5.1 *Integral Preaching and Belief*

I would now like to move from the Council to
the document "Evangelii nuntiandi" which
Paul VI. published at the end of 1975. In this
document, the quintessence of the Second
Vatican Council, as outlined before, is incor-
porated, more precisely defined and linked to
the term of "*evangelization*" as the appropriate
"terminus technicus". I would like to stress that
the Catholic understanding of "evangelization"
is quite different from the many different
meanings this term has got in the denomina-
tions and in particular movements in the
churches. For example, it must not be mixed
up with this term as it is understood within
charismatic (in the special sense) or evangelical
groups.

The term "evangelization" occurs already in
the Council texts, but in different contexts and
in any case not in this characterized terminology. For this reason, it is incorrect to suggest,
as is often done in a defensive manner, that the
term "evangelization" is imported from the
theology of liberation and comes from South

America. Evangelization is moreover a term authorized by the church's teaching itself which reconstructs the decisive dogmatic progress of the II. Vatican Council and which is unthinkable without not only the experiences of the churches in Africa and South America, but also without the European history of enlightenment within theology and of particular movements in the West-European church before the Council took place. The dogmatic term "evangelization" concentrates the findings of the Council, regarding the preaching of the Gospel in teaching *and* acting, on the basis of the church as the people of God. The self-fulfillment of the church is precisely at this point.

The South American Bishops Conference in Puebla made this paper, with the special agreement of John Paul II.,[28] to the basic document of their discussions and results, whilst in European countries it has remained relatively unnoticed. According to "Evangelii nuntiandi" (EN) one must understand the meaning of the Gospel in its entirety: evangelization does not only take place verbally or in the sacrament, but also in actions of the personal and political sphere of the Christian and the community. Nothing can be removed from the evangelizing

28 Cf. John Paul II., *Predigten und Ansprachen* (Dominikanische Republik/Mexiko 1979) ed. by the Deutsche Bischofskonferenz (Bonn 1979) p. 49.

effect of the church. "Evangelizing means for the church carrying the Good News to all areas of mankind and to change them by its influence from inside and to renew mankind itself...it would thus be most correct to say; the church evangelizes when it concerns itself, through the divine power of the message which it preaches, at the same time with the change of the personal and collective consciousness of mankind, the activity in which they are involved, their real life and present environment..." (EN No. 18). "Evangelization has to reach life.." (EN No. 47). The whole world belongs to the target area of evangelization, in particular with regard to the "righteous edification of the human community" and the "salvation of the human personality".[29] Exactly here lies the identity of the church: "Evangelization is indeed the grace and the essential, the actual calling and vocation of the church, its deepest identity" (EN No. 14).

In this statement, the identity of the church is defined by means of a purposeful process and thereby the hierarchical structural dimension and manifestation are no longer (at least, not primarily) claimed to be the absolute criteria of truth for the authenticity of the church. Here, in a criteriological process, is determined what and where the church is, which cannot be

---

29 Thus already in Gaudium et spes No.3, 43 and 45.

understood in any other way than that the hierarchy is subordinated to this criterium and has to be measured by it. However, true not only for the hierarchy, but also for the whole church, is the following: "the church, as the carrier of evangelization, is beginning to evangelize itself...The Second Vatican Council reminded us and the Synod of 1974 took up with vigour this subject of the church which evangelizes itself by constant change and renewal in order to evangelize the world in a believable way" (No. 15).

Of decisive importance is the view that the concept of evangelization is not thought of as the identity of the church solely within itself. For the church has to realize itself as an evangelizing body by realizing itself from the inside *to the outside*. For the meaning of evangelization is nothing other than the service of the church to mankind and this service is no other than the one which it realizes within itself. And only when it acts evangelically in word and deed in the way of Jesus Christ does it reach theological self-awareness of being the sacrament of salvation for the world and mankind as concrete salvation and redemption in their concrete circumstances or with the necessary changes in these circumstances. Evangelization is thus not identical to the term of Christianization which presupposes the Christianity of the church as

the producer of Christianity and the deficit of
Christianity and the need for it among the
people who do not belong to the church.
Evangelization, on the other hand, presupposes
that Christians and the church are constantly in
need of it themselves and therefore only in this
process can they encounter the need of mankind for healing participation and liberation.
The term evangelization thus means an identity
of the church which is not restricted outwardly
or inwardly, but in which it gives itself for the
salvation of all people and by this finds the way
to its own identity.

5.2 *Orientation to Christ*

The church finds its identity in being a sign and
reality of the redemption and liberation for the
world, because there exists "a merging of the
earthly and heavenly community".[30] The reason
for this is of a christological nature, as "God's
word, through which all is created, became
flesh itself to rescue all in complete humanity
and to unite the universe". E. Klinger accordingly defines this more precisely; "In evangelization, the basic formula of Christianity, the

---

30 Cf. Gaudium et spes No.40.

formula of the Council of Chalcedon, the inconfuse – indivise (unmixed and undivided, O.F.) becomes a principle of the solution of the problem of politics. This pastoral extension of christology into sociology, in my opinion, points the way and is unfortunately still unknown in Europe".[31] The Gospel and mankind belong together, unmixed and undivided in their social and worldly contexts.

Evangelization is therefore *service* for mankind and for the world and is therein (and never divided from it) the *preaching* of salvation. Furthermore, the preaching of salvation transcends in its relationship to God and in the promise of the kingdom of God, the real service to mankind and the world in two directions (it is thus not simply mixed with this service): as a release from the immense pressure of having to create the kingdom of God themselves (which mostly leads to resignation or to violence), and also as a release from hopelessness in failure and at the same time as a dynamic to never relinquish the service and liberation (with an orientation to Jesus, that is, in following him). Thereby the believed transcendence becomes deed in one's own willingness to transcend the

---

31 E. Klinger, Politik und Theologie. In: *Theologie und Glaube 71* (1981) 2 pp. 184–207, p. 185.

existing situation in the changing action of renewal.[32]

The church community or parish thus always involves itself in the preaching of salvation *as* the servant of the world and in the service of the world *as* the preacher of salvation. This takes place whenever the church is the place where people believe in the Gospel, strengthen each other in this belief *and* where people help and encourage one another to determine and notice the places (instead of repressing and keeping them quiet) where appropriate action is necessary. It is also where Christians realize the appropriate processes of action by diaconia and liberation according to their hope. The processes of change in evangelization are not only discussed, but are also dealt with. In an accurate interpretation of the christological context of reality, they have an incarnate quality, inasmuch as the word becomes flesh in the "body of Christ living on in the church" through this evangelization process. Dogmatic truths are thus not only maintained and argumentatively claimed in the spoken word, but are experienced as principles of human existence and communication. Thus, the message of redemption in the christological dogma of Chalcedon is proved true as libe-

---

32 Cf. John Paul II. 'Ansprachen' p. 64.

ration. Theology then possesses "being in this life" as it "exposes the horizons of liberation in everyday life" as the praxis of liberating and healing services for mankind and the world.[33]

This can also be formulated in terms of the kingdom-of-God-theology. The decisive duty of the church lies in the preaching of the kingdom of God and, with the help of God, to create a real existence of this kingdom in history. According to the spoken action of Jesus: when I liberate people from their conditions of oppression with the finger of my hand, when I heal their illnesses, when I show solidarity with them, when I remove their burden of guilt in the name of God and tell them of God's hope, then this is all connected with the kingdom of God (see above chapter 2.3). God's reality comes to the fore in such mercifulness and justice. The church is nothing else than the symbolic (in word and sacrament) and social (in the community and solidarity to the outside and inside) means for preaching and partial realization of the liberating "dominion" of a humane God amongst mankind. The kingdom of God means the gift of belief in a God who values all people in their personal and structural frag-

---

33 Cf. E. Klinger, Theologie im Horizont der Politik. In: S. Castillo e.a. (ed.), *Herausforderung. Die dritte Welt und die Christen Europas* (Regensburg 1980) pp. 47-63, p. 53.

mentation, who loves them unconditionally and does not desert them, even, and particularly, in death. The kingdom of God thus means the facilitating power to live, work and fight in one's individual historical and social situation for justice and solidarity.

That which the church is able to call the kingdom of God because of the biblical revelation in a way which gives hope and inspiration, goes further than the church in its factual presence. And this not only in the actions of love and justice of many people but also in many religious transcendent and non-religious symbolizations (in works of art, in the context of meditation, in poetry, in music etc.) which maintain hope in many hopeless situations, also in the ever threatening suspicion of senselessness in the risk of practically representing justice, freedom and love in this world.

In the background of this briefly mentioned kingdom-of-God-theology, evangelization is then that process in which the church does not only believe in the presence of the kingdom of God within itself, but also discovers, supports and provokes it in other forms, previously unknown to the church, in people, cultures and societies. In addition it gives the message that humanity and solidarity are not to be understood as mere laws which lead to despair or violence, but as a blessing which also sustains in loss and failure because there is a God who shows solidarity with those also showing it and who gives with his help a new beginning to those who fail or are guilty in consolation without end.

The crucial difference in the image of the church which stands to debate can perhaps be concentrated in two questions: do the people belong to the church, or is the church with the people? Is the church realized as an end in itself in that the boundaries of the kingdom of God are reduced to the boundaries of the church and the membership of the kingdom of God is strictly limited to the membership of the church? After this church-integrated and integrating model the traditional sentence would still be valid; outside the church, there is no redemption (also not beyond death). Then people who are still frightened by this can only subject themselves to the pressure of self-integration in order to take part in the reward.

There lies the fundamentalist attitude that one's own fundaments (belief, church, culture, view of life) represent as a matter of course good or at least the better, whilst other cultural and social areas are subject to the principal proviso of being bad or worse. If one views for example the relationship between church and world in such a dualistic black and white view, then the church can only produce good and the world bad. Everything which is not church can only become good or better if it commits itself to the church. The church is regarded as identical to the kingdom of God. Missionary work presents itself as a one-sided activity of the believers towards the godless. And as the "world" does not possess anything of value itself, in any case the world can be used and exploited for the aims of the church. In the instrumental use of that which the world has to offer in the way of human intelligence, energy, technology and media, then one does no longer need to be petty. But such an instrumental use (better, misuse) of the "world" merely for the sake of the church and its powerful influence is countereffective to the service of the church for the sake of the world destroying the possibility to communicate with the world in a dialogical and appreciating way.

5.3 *The Competence of the Basis*

If one can describe the identity of the church in this way as a *process* of evangelization, then preaching can no longer be reduced to the "authorized" preaching of the ministers in word and sacrament, although this is still indispensable (naturally in the communicative exchange with all Christians and charismata).

When the "underdogs" of society are themselves the location of the presence of the "above" (of the Gospel of the Son of God), then this has consequences for a new definition of those responsible for this evangelization.

The church cannot take it for granted "that its message is restricted only to the religious area by not interesting itself for the current problems of mankind" (EN No.34). Thus one cannot be told often and expressly enough that evangelization does not stop with preaching and the explanation of teaching. For evangelization must reach life, the individual and social life; only then does this life reach the horizon of the Gospel and it will be opened in itself for the supernatural life, which is not the negation, but the transfiguration and intensification of natural life (cf. EN No.47). Thus it is true to say: "the whole church is therefore called to evangelization and thus there are different tasks within it which are to be fulfilled in the service of the conveying of belief" (EN No.66).

Decisive statements from the Council are thus included in the precise context of the term "evangelization". Here one has to consider particularly the inclusion of the theology of the *charismata* in the ecclesiogical conception of the church as the holy people of God, as well as the christological determination and simultaneous integration of the *service* for the preaching of

100

redemption (and for believing in it) *and* for the humanization of the world (where both the latter occur in the Council documents unfortunately as relatively independent next to one another sometimes divided between the preaching services of the ministers and the "worldly" services of the lay people).[34] Accordingly, evangelization is a *communal* duty of both lay people and ministers (and here not divided anymore between service for the world and service for the redemption). Only the whole parish can be the basis of this reality-orientated preaching, inasmuch as it has a social relevance for both the edification of the parish and for the improvement of the social environment. Those who wish to realize that "new way of life, of communal life which the Gospel opens up" form a community "which is itself a sign of change, a sign of new life; the church, the visible sacrament of salvation" (EN No.23). Therefore, "out of the need to experience the life of the church more intensively, or out of the wish or the search for a personal atmosphere which the large parishes cannot offer" smaller church communities form, in which the individual life and the life with the church and society are

---

34 Compare for example Lumen Gentium No. 12 and No. 33 with No. 31.

discussed amongst themselves based on the Gospel and in prayer to God (cf. EN No.58).

All believers are principally theologically indispensable with their specific charismata for the processes of evangelization as well as they are indispensable in the self-experience of the parish as responsible and necessary participants: Firstly, the believers need each other in order to perceive adequately what is going on, to communicate with one another and to analytically comprehend the *reality*. They need each other, secondly, to discuss the revelation in the written word and tradition as the source of their hope, their solidarity and their change in praxis and in such *remembrance* to allow their individual charismata to be realized for the explanation of biblical and theological sources. Thirdly, the believers need each other in order to talk together about the *change* in their ways, to conceive it in the various stages, to organize corresponding action and thus become, in the area of their situation for themselves and others, a place of humanity and salvation. For these *three steps of diaconia* (which, of course, often occur within each other and mixed up together) of seeing, judging and acting on the horizon of a Gospel which is collectively remembered and is realized in change, an ecclesiology can only be valid in which the charismata of all are required (also in their one-sidedness and thus in their individual abilities) and which forms the church in the unity and supplementation with one another (see for further explanation below chapter 8).

Two *abilities* will have particularly close contact with one another within the *"seeing"* of diaconia. *Firstly* perception accompanied with mercifulness *and secondly* analysis orientated to social justice, so that individual help does not become stabilizing therapy of the political or social system and so that, conversely, the structural criticism does not lose sight of the suffering and treats them without compassion. Christian diaconia should never come under suspicion of perpetuating the structural conditions through its abstinence in the field of political diaconia, by treating the problems and therapizing them only caritatively. In this context, one must reflect more exactly on the specific processes of diaconical action, between actions of help on one hand *and* social or economic criticism on the other, in their mutual relationship and support.

One could provisionally envisage these two *steps* of diaconia (concerning seeing and doing under the guidance of the Gospel): 1. The direct perception of human need *and* the analysis of its individual and structural existence and origins (seeing), 2. liberating actual and long-term action of help (with lasting patience) for the suffering (which improves their individual and structural situation now) *and* at the same time socio-political involvement which takes sides with appropriate social as well as political competence (doing).

Options based on social factors are to be defined in this sense individually and structurally. The term "option" pertains to the Latin American Theology of Liberation and means in no way something, which is optional, but precisely the opposite. "Option" means decisive priorities, which have to be understood hermeneutically in the sense of the Magnificat especially: "He has exalted these of low degree... He has filled the hungry with good things." (Lk I,52-53) and: "He has regarded the low estate of his handmaiden." (Lk I,48). That means: all, who enjoy no priorities at all, but are disadvantaged and below, are the hermeneutical and real basis in finding options, in order that they become "exalted". This is according to the will of God. Whoever, however, gives priorities to the ones who enjoy them already, so that they become even richer and more powerful at the expense of the poor, decides options, which are against God's will, who is going to send the rich away empty and to degrade the mighty.

The most crucial problem in this context is however, how the competence of the supposed incompetent, how the importance of the un-

important people is guaranteed *structurally.*
Which institutions have to be established, so
that the disadvantaged get their advantage to
speak up? If we do not change the corresponding structures, then nothing will happen.

I would like to display this problem in the
field of church ministry. The ministers of the
church have their power for the sake of the
powerless. It is their duty therefore to care for
the structural possibilities that suffering people
have something to say in the church. They
need not only to speak instead of them or
merely advocate them, but they have to provide
the institutional facilities in which the disadvantaged people can speak about their lives
and needs. It is an integral part of the official
ministry of teaching and preaching that the
ministers know, that there are two *sources* of
Christian preaching the Gospel: firstly, not to
forget the stories of revelation in the past, in the
tradition, especially of course in the Bible. And,
secondly, not to forget the people in the
present, who are suffering and who are deprived of rights. For the real encounter with them
is the condition of the possibility to understand
the stories of the past as stories of victims
themselves and to discover that the kingdom of
God is especially for them and has to reach
them by means of the church: following the
most important victim according to the Chris-

tian belief, Jesus himself, who became a victim because he had shown solidarity with victims.

The decision towards an option in the highly complex processes of industrialized and computerized societies is not an easy one, especially if concrete situations are concerned. One cannot always formulate an option in general terms (as for a whole country, for example), but often only in contact with specific experiences of need in the place itself (with the unemployed, where their number is particularly increasing, with young people, where they are particularly in danger of drug abuse, with the refugees etc.). Only based on such partially recognized social problems can interregional options be discussed. The social contradictions have to be discovered in a particular place and in detail, which are easily distorted or even hidden by the global view of a society. Of course, conversely, structural analyses of interregional contexts must be applied to experiences of need which are confined to one area.

5.4 *From the Many Words to the Decisive Deed*

Maybe it is true that words are the church's weakest resource. But how does the great arsenal of words (both those in the area of the church's teaching as well as those in the texts of the Jewish-Christian tradition) come into the realm of deed? For that which is the decisive action in the respective situation and for which we have the necessary competence and energy, there are, of course, too many verbal statements than that which we are able and have to put into action in the course of our lives. We are already limited by our corporeality and the limitation of presence forced on us by it, but also by the limitation of the length of our life and by our specific possibilities and impossibilities. The recognition of this limitation also belongs to our existence as human beings, if we do not want to play at being gods. Thus the relationship of word and deed in individual people, but also in groups of Christians, in the parish and in the religious communities cannot be imagined in any other way than in the image of a funnel, through which only a small amount of the many words can reach their practical realization as they pass down the tapered section of it. If the contact of word and deed happens in our life, then we are forced to make it in limited actions and limited places. It is important in the life of Christians, of the parish and of the religious orders to set one's own priorities in this process (because one cannot do everything), then, however, to see the chosen action through with the necessary consistency.

In the concept of evangelization such a

decisiveness in the goal of a person or of a community has to be called "option" again. Therefore this term must not be misunderstood as an oversized and excessive term of achievement but takes the reality and the limitation of the charismata seriously, as it also responds to definite challenges of the personal and social situation and at the same time concentrates itself on them. With reference to Jesus, we see that he allowed himself in his options to be determined especially from the situation of the oppressed, the disadvantaged and the suffering. Without doubt, the experiences of need of those affected have an outstanding prerogative to provoke the charismata of Christians and to be brought into contact with them. Thus an option combines in a humane way the Indicative of the personal and communal possibilities and the Imperative of the situational and historical challenges. Necessary exertion in praxis and the necessary limitation in engagement need each other, so that, at least in one area, sometimes like a drop in the ocean, word becomes deed. The term "option" also combines eschatologically the tension and release (from total demands of the super-ego) of the "Yes, already" and the "Not yet" of the kingdom of God within our history.

When the biblical prophets speak out then they never speak in an arbitrary way (concerning praxis) of the will of Yahweh, rather they say unmistakably that the belief in Yahweh and his choice of Israel and his word are only compatible with a specific religious, social and political praxis (see above chapter 2.3). It becomes clear that the prophetic process is sparked off at the moment when the determination of options occurs in the concept of evangelization. Within evangelization, the option determines that which is the concrete precision and unyielding nature of the biblical prophecy; prophecy, in the sense if this prophetic process within evangelization represents an inalienable characteristic of the church's identity and existence. For the decision of priority is mentioned within it where in view of the position and time (of the individual, community, town, country, part of the world) an urgency of a specific action exists of a type which allows no deviation. Other matters become of secondary importance but not absolutely so, as in other situations and times they too may enter the horizon of priority.

The term "option" is therefore a term of criticism against any pastoral care of a global nature, which wants to achieve and pursue everything possible, but does not tackle that which is decisive in a particular situation (in particular, in situations of need). This insight relieves us from the ever-present pressure of quantity which is in our hearts and minds and replaces it with quality through limited quantity. Christians will not be able to do more in this present "eon" (age) if they really believe that the complete kingdom of God can only penetrate our history with the coming of Jesus Christ. Our quantitive ideas of the super-ego have nothing to do with evangelization. I believe that this is a completely redeeming and liberating message for all those responsible within the church.

The term "option" is often accused of unduly narrowing the "fullness" and "universality" of the revelation, in that it reduces the "free" or "neutral" reception of the Gospel by a preliminary decision. The "option for the poor" is accused therefore of being a pauperism because the rich no longer appear as the target group of the revelation. Didn't Jesus die for all and hasn't he redeemed everyone? The latter is of course correct, but does not include the fact that everyone may read and receive the Bible as he or she wants. Precisely when the Gospel is applicable for all (and not in general terms, but concrete), then their different situations must integrate into the communication with the revelation and must be made clear in it, so that they can be really reached as they are. The poor and the rich will be allowed or will have to identify themselves in the biblical texts with those as they occur there (for example, as the poor referred to in the first Beatitude or as the rich in the story of the rich young man). From this viewpoint, the option for the poor corresponds exactly to the "option for the rich", that the latter accept the Gospel when they follow Jesus in his message of change for the benefit of the poor and thus free themselves from their fear concerning their possessions and power (that is, from their spiritual "poverty").

Options are from this perspective the discovery of situations and people of the present in the stories and figures of the Bible, in order to activate the relationships which are related and shown favourably there between people and God or among people for a concretely defined and often also innovative recalling of the message. The options for the reception of biblical models (but also of dogmas) are thereby neither unlimited nor arbitrary. After all, the important issue for the determination of options is a decisive goal which does not make the church's other areas of praxis redundant, but also realizes itself in these and takes its power from them (particularly in the service in prayers for the suffering and to obtain the power to help them and bear the risks of solidarity).

6. The Service of God and the Service of Mankind

6.1 Essential Realizations of the Church

A more precise definition of the three basic functions of the church[35] (koinonia, martyria and diaconia; community, preaching and service) and their relation to each other is given from the perspective of evangelization. This concern for the basic functions of the church *identifies* the areas of action of the church in the *theological* concept of evangelization as well as in its systematic principles and practical consequences. In such a deeper definition, the reference to biblical terminology and events seems to be theologically more legitimate. The principal determination of the relationship between diaconia and martyria on the horizon of

---

35 As R. Zerfaß formulated them in 1974 based on S.Hiltner's classification which had been raised by human science before it was associated with corresponding phenomena occurring in the New Testament. See R. Zerfaß, Praktische Theologie als Handlungswissenschaft. In: F. Klostermann/Id. (ed.), *Praktische Theologie heute* (München/Mainz 1974) pp. 164–177.

evangelization also allows koinonia to appear more differentiated.

Although the basic functions are three or four dimensional (with liturgy), *martyria* (as verbal and sacramental preaching of the love of God) and *diaconia* (as the love of one's neighbour through justice and mercy) epitomise christological qualities of evangelization in a different way than koinonia, the life of Christians in their communities and parishes. Both cannot do without koinonia and both cannot remain together without koinonia! Koinonia is the communal social ground or sphere of orthodoxy and orthopraxy, of the service of God and the service of mankind, of martyria and diaconia, of kerygmatic-sacramental and diaconical mission for and with each other. The three dimensions, however, do not lie on the same level, as they are not of the same constituitive category. The church community has the character of being service for the sake of the relationship of God and mankind *and* for the sake of improving relationships within mankind. Koinonia can only do this when *it is determined* in its purpose-related structure *by martyria and diaconia*. This shows and makes possible all the more that its intrinsic value lies totally within this christological identity, that is, proclaiming and presenting the Gospel of the redeeming God for all people and the liberating love of mankind through its own actions. Jesus sought the encounter and the company of people to give them his healing and liberating help and to proclaim the evidence of the merciful God and his kingdom within this real diaconia.

In effect then, there are "only" two *fundamental* dimensions to the existence of the church, at least on the horizon of the concept of evangelization: martyria and diaconia, which can never be realized outside the corresponding koinonia. However, koinonia must be more closely defined by the condition that it realizes the martyria and diaconia authentically. Only then materializes in koinonia the fundamental equality of all people and the reciprocity of all charismata so that nobody is entitled to produce dependencies from top to bottom in that the communication of words is conveyed as a ruling knowledge or the communication with people in need degrades the others to being mere objects of giving help.

Naturally, one cannot assume that every Christian and each Christian social form fulfil both the basic functions of word and deed thoroughly and equally. This would be an abstraction of the real possibilities and of a concrete, individual and collective theology of charismata.

By the term "collective charismata", I understand the fact that Christians join together, in a group or institution, with charismata directed in a similar way (for example, towards the "option" of a particular social work, again with different abilities and qualifications) in order to act more effectively and with more solidarity for others within this social form of the church. In such koinonia, they attain a new quality which goes beyond the individual charismata, as a church which is on the spot. Thus I maintain the legitimate partiality, the one-sidedness and the dominance of the presence of the Gospel in different social forms. The verbal and sacramental or the diaconical presence of Christ is made possible in the church, precisely by the *fact* that both are manifested by means of different charismata and different communities all the more intensively for the necessary "one-sided" recalling of Christ *and*, at the same time *that* both ensure that they remain in contact. If the "division of labour" in the church does not collapse into sectoral separation and loss of relationship, then it is ecclesiologically legitimate and can justifiably be a socio-structural expression of the christological "unmixed" combination of the service of God and the service of mankind in the church.

6.2 *Synopsis*

The model suggested here of the areas of presence of evangelization or basic functions of the church can be depicted in the following diagram:

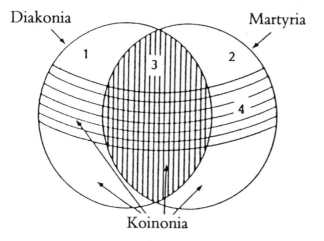

The overlapping circles represent the two basic dimensions of diaconia and martyria (in word and sacrament). In both, there are independent areas (1 and 2) such as the particular connection between diaconia and sociology (for the empirical analysis of social factors), as well as with the human sciences which make qualified help possible. The relatively independent areas in martyria would be such areas as discussions of belief, the sermon, the liturgy, but also academic theology (with the appropriate partnerships of knowledge with philosophy, literature and linguistic science, for example). In these specific and characteristic areas of both dimensions the other area is also necessary, but is only *implicitly* contained within it, in the condition of its being in another aggregation: Thus, a theology which reflects the dimension of diaconia in it will come to different results than if it develops only according to apologetic arguments. Conversely, a special diaconical spirituality realizes itself in a particular fashion on the basis of diaconical actions inasmuch as the relationship to Christ is experienced in the encounter with the suffering.

In many areas of life and deed, both dimensions will overlap each other as they are expressed in each other and *explicitly* "manifested" (3): when, for example, in a conventional parish (which normally concentrates on liturgical services, sermons and faith) social work groups are formed which realize the dimension of diaconia. Conversely, in a diaconical institution, its own theology will become explicit when its members (its social workers and their target groups) learn to speak to one another about their faith in real contact. Diaconia then incorporates martyria explicitly into itself when those involved in social care talk about their Christian motivation with each other and with the people they care for. In this area of the explicit realization of the relationship between diaconia and martyria, both areas of presence of the church learn how they live and exist within one another.

An entire congruence of both areas (= circles) everytime and everywhere would be overtaxing and need not be postulated! The band which encircles both circles (4) shows the communication of exchange between both areas as they both learn to discover and value each other and also discover themselves in the other area. Here, the moments which otherwise belong to the independent areas of each dimension (1 and 2) come into contact with each other. In this band, too, much has to be communicated between the two dimensions, so that one may come to know the other from the dimension which is missing explicitly from the praxis in one's own area and life. This is important particularly because no-one and also no social form is able to realize everything due to the limited charismata of an individual and collective nature.

Let me now return from this point in my survey to koinonia. It realizes itself here fourfold; as koinonia in both the areas of the basic functions of the church "concerned with themselves" (1 and 2), then in the area of encounter (3) where one explicitly expresses or realizes the dimension of the other area in one's own and thereby provokes the possibility and necessity to establish contact with each other for the sake of mutual interest. That happens in the communication which encircles both areas (4) in which one hears from the other area, values its matter of concern, bears it with solidarity and discovers it within oneself at the same time as a matter of concern which, however, one cannot or will not *practically* follow oneself. The unity of diaconia and martyria is perceived, experienced and seen as important in the real koinonia amongst each other. Such determinations of the relationship of diaconia and martyria together and in each other refer to all scales and levels of their realization: on the level of the diocese and charity organization, the presbytery and social institution, the bible group and social circle (in the parish), of different individual persons and within the same person concerning his or her different phases in life.

6.3 *Diaconical Responsibility for the Church's Ministers*

From the perspective of diaconia, a characteristic social responsibility for the formation of the parish lies with the church officials and particularly the ordained ministers. It is a duty here which has a "hierarchical" quality inasmuch as it does not derive from the democratic majority but stands in "opposition" to this in a prophetic and critical way. For the civic majority of the parish can be so orientated that they do not allow the minority to have its say or even suppress it. The minorities I speak of here are those which realize the diaconical relationship with those affected and support corresponding political options or are themselves affected. In such conflicts between the majority which is distanced from diaconia and a minority which is close to it, between the "church from below" (democratically) and the "church which is totally down below" (socially), the church ministers have to flex their "hierarchical" muscles for the good of the latter and use their structural power for the sake of the powerless. On this horizon the church's teaching is understandable as that the first and last basis of the church is not based on the democratic paradigm but on the paradigm of the "kingdom of God" (which is given in the revelation) where the hungry are given food and the rich are sent away empty, where the lowly are raised up and the powerful are brought down (cf. Lk 1,51-53).

If one takes this option for the sake of minorities into the definition of democracy that there should be no social contradictions within it and that, as long as this is not the case, the increasing importance of the poor is represented, then there should be no tension between fundamental democratizing and fundamental option. For then such an understanding of democracy contains itself the tendency towards social justice. In any case, the aforementioned tension must be thematized in order to avoid misunderstandings whether the discussion be in the understanding of democracy itself or between the terms democracy and option.

If the church administration understands reality from the perspective of the poor and interprets from this standpoint the "sign of the times", then it becomes open to criticism that it ignores the rich in all this. However, just the opposite is the case. A bishop in Brazil formulated it so: "Of course I go to the rich, but I go to them after I've been to the poor. I visit the rich from the perspective of the poor!" The option for the poor prevents them being grouped together with the rich as if the preaching of the Gospel could "pass over their heads" unaware of their specific situation. The option does not select the rich out, but makes clear their structural position in the real social life and thereby their social duty in evangelization. Thus it is not an option against the rich, rather this option cares for them as the message reaches them according to their specific role which they take in the real circumstances. Whoever wishes to keep these circumstances out of the Christian faith also keeps evangelization out of social contradictions and its history and reduces it to arbitrary words (see above chapter 5.4).

The definition of justice, mercifulness or humanity is best established from the standpoint of those who have to experience their lack personally and structurally. If one tries to define these terms separate from those affected, then they are deprived of their own interests. If the church administration learns to live and think from the viewpoint of the affected (like the USA bishops, for example, in their bishop's letter of 1986)[36] then the outlook on life and people gradually alters and becomes radical, then the way of leadership in the parishes also alters. The suffering do not only have a right to be helped but also have something important to say! The church ministry should make sure that in a Christian community the suffering always have the right to have their say and this particularly in the presence of those believers who are deaf in this respect. It should be understood that the church ministry should not speak only as in a lobby for the affected but also that minis-

---

36 Cf. N.Mette, Die kirchliche und politische Dimension der Caritas, in: H.Bogensberger/W.Zauner (ed.), *Perspektiven des Sozialstaates 2000* (St. Pölten-Wien 1990) pp. 53-66.

try works for social forms beyond such ambivalent caring where the affected may speak themselves. The so-called social "periphery" has a great meaning for the "centre" and qualifies its real relationship to the Gospel. This will make more trust and willingness to cooperation on the part of the affected because they learn the importance of their lives and survival through social recognition and participating integration.

In the West-European churches and parishes, one must warn of fluently speaking of a "theology of liberation" and of "basic communities". As an example: even when democratic equality of all those baptized in our parishes is realized, this would not be a basic community as it is understood on the other side of the "Big Pond". For the basis there is not primarily characterized by these civic demands for freedom but by people in need and injustice (as well as by people who show solidarity with them), who take their own fate into their hands, define their situation according to the Gospel and organize their actions with the corresponding demands for liberation.

Who else should have the primary power of definition of justice than those who are the victims of injustice? There is no liberation which acts above their heads and hearts. Or to put it biblically: without listening to the message of the poor (here, disadvantaged people in general) there is no praxis of the Gospel, because otherwise the kingdom of God does not set foot in the destructive conflicts of history.

Whoever wishes to preach the Gospel to the poor can only do so if he puts himself in a position where the poor themselves determine the liberating manifestation of the Gospel. For this reason there is also, alongside the official church ministry for preaching, something like an equivalent unofficial "ministry for preaching" of those who live in need and injustice. If the preaching of the hierarchy "from above" does not seek this preaching of the hierarchy "from below" then the history of suffering and liberation in the Jewish-Christian tradition cannot be effectively linked with the suffering in the present for the sake of their liberation. Therefore the spiritual and prophetic duty of the church official ministry lies in allowing and encouraging the prophetic and political preaching of the poor to take place: for their words are in fact connected with God, who wants them to be liberated.

For in the same way as the remembrance of the suffering and their liberation constitutes the horizon of the biblical belief in God, as tradition tells it, the stories of suffering and their liberation of the present are also not subject to a bourgeois democratic process, but have an implicit requirement for help and thus their need within themselves. A majority which is not at the same time representative of the perspective of the affected cannot decide on their existence and their obligatory claim. The stories of the victims are to be realized in a privileged way and taken seriously for the existence of the Christian and the church: in liberating love and solidarity with them. One cannot decide upon the existence of past and present cases of victims and liberation by means of quantitative power (not even by the "power of the people"): moreover not one jot of their stories or complaints should go astray. Only the word of the sufferers and people showing solidarity in the present gives the word of the people in the past who have suffered and shown solidarity its importance related to the present in a practical way. We have to discover that this direct connection to the poor belongs directly to the formation on the church. In many cases this "other half" of the preaching is somewhat missing.

Therefore the vital importance of suffering and disadvantaged people for the development of the church community must be brought to the fore against any superficial egality: not everyone has the claim to the same importance (in the ignorance of their different social status and personal situation). Moreover, the poor of the past and present have not only as much to say as the rich, but they have more to say than these others. Only that is the condition for the possibility that they are put on the same level as the others. One must listen to their descriptions and analyses of their situations as well as their stories and demands for change. Such a listening process has the holistic character of sharing life; in this way the church realizes itself. Otherwise it loses life and sinks back into the boredom of the insignificant because it has no direct contact with concrete need and is therefore not needed! Also the needs of the Christians themselves sometimes have too little influence on the manner and way of community building. The competence for the diaconical way of life begins in the accepted plurality and perception of need in its own house (see below chapter 8).

Decisive for all this is the universality of the aforementioned competence of the poor: all poor people have this obligatory advantage due to their practical experience of need, not only the poor who belong to the Christian ranks. Such a right of the disadvantaged to receive attention cannot be split. Only the realization of this fact frees the church from the allures of indoctrination and authoritarianism and constitutes a liberating Catholicism, freeing itself from unnecessary limitations. Then the church risks a transition "beyond itself" which does the world good.

6.4 *The Fruitful Tension between Fellowship and Service*

If we see the problem in this light, then the concept of "brotherly love" is surely insufficient to cover "Church for others". It may also be too undifferentiated, since it does not distinguish clearly enough between *koinonia* (the fellowship of believers) and *diaconia* (service to the suffering, including strangers and opponents, which continually tears down the barriers of the "internal" fellowship). Moreover, brotherly love all too easily suggests that service for others is exhausted in service for "the brethren".[37] But in fact fellowship towards the inside and service towards the outside stand in considerable tension to one another, in terms both of social psychology and institutional theory; for no interest group willingly puts someone at the

37 Cf. K. Lehmann, Nochmals: Caritas und Pastoral. In: *Caritas 88* (1987) pp. 1,3-12, where it is not really clear where the main reference of the brotherly and ministering congregation lies. The general trend of the argument would suggest that it is koinonia rather than diaconia. This is shown, for example, by the use of the term 'all' in the following quotation: 'All are there for one another. All are members of the one body' (p. 9). On the mutual delimitation between koinonia and diaconia, and their critical complementation, cf., also R. Zerfaß, *Der Beitrag des Caritasverbandes zur Diakonie der Gemeinde.* In: *Caritas 88* (1987) pp. 1,12-27, 19ff., 22ff.

centre who does not "belong", or hold the same opinions.

This tension will not emerge, however, if service is made over to a separate church organization, as in the churches in Germany (which is the "Caritasverband" in the Catholic Church and the "Diakonisches Werk" in the Protestant Church).[38] The parishes then feel that they have been relieved of this task. If we look at the resulting practice, in the church's *koinonia* (fellowship) and *diaconia* (service for others), we see that there really is unconditional ministry for all the suffering and oppressed; but this is confined largely to the initiatives and institutions of the church's charitable associations. The Caritas, for example has 28,000 institutions (hospitals, homes for the handicapped, social and counselling centres, etc.) and 300,000 full time workers, thereby being the largest charitable organization in West Germany.[39] But these initiatives

---

38 Cf. H.Steinkamp, Diakonia in the Church of the Rich and the Church of the Poor: A comparative Study in Empirical Theology. In: *Concilium 24* (1988) pp. 65-75.

39 The institutions of the freely sponsored welfare organisations (the sponsor in this case being the church) are 80 per cent financed by the state, the rest having to be supplied by the church from its own income (which results from church tax and voluntary contributions). Persons employed in the parishes and in special sectors of pastoral care amount to only about 20 per cent of the number employed in the Caritas

and institutions are relatively cut off from the parishes. Consequently the parishes could and can without embarrassment concentrate on "more essential" sectors of passing on the faith, through proclamation in word and sacrament. So in over 50 per cent of West German parishes, service for others plays a highly reduced role, generally as a particular topic on special collection Sundays.[40] The other 50 per cent (especially the student congregations) are increasingly and unerringly sensitive to and aware of local needs. They concern themselves with the possible organization of help and with supra-regional solidarity actions. Though here, certainly, local parishes should watch more carefully to see how far service is limited to believers. For example, does a Catholic kindergarten accept the children of immigrant Turkish workers?

---

organization! But the corresponding awareness among those employed full-time in pastoral care and in theology is certainly in inverse proportion to this representation of the church's ministry in society; for among theologians and those concerned in pastoral care, the church's expression of itself through service is seldom discussed. On the history and development of the Caritasverband, and on its relationship to the congregations, cf. R.Zerfaß, Organisierte Caritas als Herausforderung an eine nachkonziliare Theologie. In: E. Schulz, H. Brosseder and H. Wahl (ed.), *Den Menschen nachgehen* (St. Ottilien 1978) pp. 321-348.

40 See Lehmann '*Caritas*' pp. 6ff.

This state of affairs cannot be considered satisfactory. The practice of the parishes is often considered legitimate, because the charitable organizations exist. But if the parishes make themselves primarily places for liturgical celebration and confessional ideology in the sphere of an ecclesiastically accepted religiosity and morality, they delegate the concerns of diaconical service (if they even know what these concerns are) to some other institution, away from the congregation; and this authority "represents" the congregation to all those in need. The parish certainly pays highly for this delegation in financial terms. But it is saved from *direct encounter* with those affected.

This "organizing away" of people who are in need and on the fringes of society has catastrophic effects for the build-up of the congregation itself, as well as for the needy, the oppressed and underprivileged, in the area served by a given parish. For the problem of professional charity is that it easily estimates – and underestimates – as dilettante, any non-professional, spontaneous, simple, everyday, matter of course, effective ways of helping by "lay" people, or their ability for service.[41] Yet without the "infrastructure" of minds orientated towards living with the affected, and the corre-

---

41 See Steinkamp 'Diakonia' p. 70ff.

sponding communicative reality of a wider social network, the highly cultivated professionalism of the charitable organization is left in the air of specialist care and treatment, which is insufficiently carried over and continued in ordinary everyday life.

For example, the hospital treatment offered by the state and charitable organizations is highly necessary, especially for those suffering from AIDS in its acute stages; yet it proves relatively helpless when it comes down to the social contexts to which people with AIDS return, in their often relatively long symptom-free periods – whether they can live there in dignity (that is, accepted and perceived as important for others), and whether they can discuss their situation, master it or endure it. The best counselling or care remains an unrelated experience unless there are also special, alternative social forms on an intermediary level (between family and the major social structures) in which those affected are not exposed to social discrimination but are given jobs, support and places to live. And the local churches would belong precisely to this "between" level.

Moreover, only the lived sensibility for service of Christians and congregations can probably perceive the need which lives beyond the zones of need defined by the charitable organisations, and outside the receiver-range accepted by the financial bureaucracy. The problems "the welfare state" has about accepting "the new poverty" in the highly industrialized countries belongs here; though the real experience of the people concerned make this poverty undeniable.

Because there is so little social contact with the handicapped, the distressed, and those suffering from discrimination, we lose the particular "competences" which these people have to offer and can claim, for a perception of what the Gospel means and for the beginnings of a practical realization of the kingdom of God. Practised service always changes the witness itself, which is to say the proclamation of the Gospel; for learning how to think and live from people who are suffering means that the practice of faith is changed and radicalized, in the context of options that are no longer optional but quite literally necessary – born of need. The suffering do not merely have a claim to help; they always have something important to say as well. That is surely why Jesus does not merely put a child in the midst, as the object of helpful service (because "not yet being grown up" counts as a deficiency); he makes children the actual yardstick for "grown ups" in their dealings with the kingdom of God (cf. Mt 19, 13-14).

Here we can discover possible ways of learning, ways we can hope for, particularly in encounters with the suffering; for the helpers help those who need it and, anticipating that the suffering can help them, accept help in their turn. This help takes the form of disquieting, yet ultimately salutary questions put to their own forms of living, their attitudes, their suppression of weakness and powerlessness, their perhaps pathologising and alienating forms of behaviour, structures and ideologies. The person who suffers always has an essentially critical, transforming and intensifying quality for all concerned.

What is in question here, therefore, is not a new moralization of service. It simply means being encouraged to expect and accept, even in such encounters – and there especially – a decisive message about more humane living. The "complementary community" comes about only in the mutual fellowship of helpers and those who need help, the healthy and the sick, the strong and the weak, where roles can be exchanged and where their possibilities and impossibilities do not have to be either left unused or suppressed, but can be "lumped together" to provide the great opportunity for a more humane church.[42]

---

42 See U. Bach, *Boden unter den Füßen hat keiner* (Göttingen 1980) pp. 70-83.

7. The Two "Natures" of the Church

7.1 Social (and) Pastoral Care[43]

In order to prevent a serious misunderstanding which the model given above (see above chapter 6.2) could give rise to without further comment on my part, I would like to stress that *both* areas realize the redeeming or *saving* function of the church in the world, with it and for it and should not under any circumstances be divided from each other between "profane service" or "holy service". Thus in the verbal and sacramental martyria, the healing (diaconical) service of Christ is also present in word. Thus, in the real diaconia, the resurrected Lord is also made present in the suffering and the helping. Diaconia is in analogous "perichoresis" just as much a holy and divine service as the benevolent Jesus as a human being is the redeemer and Son of

---

43 The conception of this term can be found in N. Mette, Sozialpastoral, in: P. Eicher/id. (ed.), *Auf der Seite der Unterdrückten?* (Düsseldorf 1989) pp. 234–265.

God.[44] Valid for *both* forms of the realization of evangelization in several parts of the church is the basic structure of the sacramental constitution of the church as the one prime and original sacrament of salvation for the world, when it allows the offer of the belief in a loving God and the experience of his love (of mankind) in the social behaviour of Christians to be "indicatively" experienced.

This view can base itself not least on the ecclesiology which is orientated on Paul's theology of charismata with its mutual dependence, which is to be realized in koinonia, of "carriers of charismata" or "charismata groups". One-sided charismata are then not only legitimate, but also necessary when they complement each other (also critically), interchange and thereby dispense salvation and liberation not only in the teaching but also in praxis. The completeness of following Jesus is not easily possible in the comparison of each of us or our communities with the entire model of Jesus, but is guaranteed in a just as happily relieving as compelling way by the assembled serving of the

---

44 The term "communicatio idiomatum" in christology means that what you are able to attribute to the one nature (human) of Christ, you can also attribute to the other (divine): for example, if Jesus died on the cross, then the Son of God died on the cross; or: if Mary is the mother of Jesus, then she is mother of God's son.

136

different individual and collective charismata as supplements: in such a composition they realize the church as the entire "body" of Christ (cf. 1 Cor 11-12).

Preaching and diaconia are related to each other in an analogous way as the "two natures" of Jesuanic, ecclesiastical and Christian existence, and are undivided and unmixed in a relational (not identical) unity. Of course, preaching is always a *service* of word, but it is not the *same* as helping and liberating deeds. For this reason, preaching cannot be interchanged with deed, and, of course, cannot replace it. Only when one keeps both areas apart are they able to criticize one another and to break up ideologizing identifications: when the minister preaches, then this is not all; above all, that is by a long way not diaconia itself; not by a long chalk. Maintaining the word is not yet doing it. When the nurse carries out her duties, then this is not yet identical with her belief and with the preaching of the word. The actions of both have the same value, but are not the same and need the respective supplementing of themselves (with regard to their own identity as well as the ecclesiatic identity through the charismata of the other).

If I consider diaconia and caritas here as a theologian I carry out *theology* and do not think for one minute that this process is already identical with diaconia itself. My explicit diaconical action is located elsewhere. This does not exclude the fact that, within theology, there is also a diaconical component inasmuch as theology thematically concerns itself for diaconia or inasmuch as within the consensus of Christians, the latter help each other in their *belief*, give fresh heart to one another and strengthen each other (as in Bible groups or discussions of faith, for example). However, such diaconia *in* martyria is again something different than diaconia *within* diaconia; as a disabled person is not (only) helped by encouragement in his belief, but (also) by the necessary physical help and social equality.

As the integral term of evangelization also permeates the definition of pastoral action, the latter must also incorporate diaconical action. This means in such a context of evangelization and of Christian action defined by it, not only spiritual welfare, but also social, individual and physical welfare. Also, not only verbal preaching in the service and conversations of spiritual welfare, but also diaconical action in a healing community and in the liberation of the oppressed, in help for those in need and in solidarity with all who are disadvantaged. The lack of warmth and sincerity in the church's pastoral care is based in many cases on its abstraction of how people are and also that faith is only

138

understood, to a great extent, spiritually, in thought or institutionally and occurs and grows too rarely as an event which can be discovered particularly in an integral encounter. This happens, on the one hand, between people and God where God becomes human and where the human being may pray "Protect and heal us in body and soul" and on the other hand, among people where there is not spiritual welfare without physical and social welfare. This starts with the access to all places in the church for those in wheelchairs and leads to the sensitive perception of physical signs and reactions of people in their faces, gestures and demeanours as well as to the corresponding reaction to them.

7.2 *The Scope of Service in the Community of the Church*

Service for others provokes the breaking down of barriers in two directions, permanently stripping faith of its ideological character, and dissolving institutional restrictions. Barriers *inwards* are broken down, because people who are in need belong from the outset to the centre of the church and to its special sphere of responsibility, simply *because* they are in need (not, for example, because they "belong"). Barriers *outwards* are destroyed when Christians and church work together with all non-Christian initiatives and groups, and with all men and women of good will, showing solidarity with those who – in their actions and in their siding with those who suffer, at home and abroad – aim to expose and combat social-political and economic causes of distress.

This dynamic, truly communicative exchange process between Church and society in the service which bridges the two, is the mark showing that christian and church manifest their identity *through* service. The universality of service to people inside and outside, in and between church and society is the historical and the specific, situational expression of the church's character as universal sacrament for the world. This universality of salvation in ministry as a whole means the criticism of all manifestations of the church which, content with their own dynamic (and understandably enough, psychologically) try to fence themselves off, and if necessary to exclude "outsiders". This is so especially in the spheres where people only meet in liturgy and worship, or where faith only seeks to assure of its doctrinal truth or moral standards.

Accordingly, while claiming unlimited scope outwards, wherever there is distress, ministry (diaconia) claims the same scope inwardly too, in a special sense: that is, within the community

140

(koinonia) of the church's own social forms. To deny divorced and remarried people admission to the sacraments is in this light behaviour hostile to ministry in the liturgical sphere (or in the conditions for admission to the sacraments laid down by canon law). Equally hostile to ministry is the longstanding contemptuous treatment of applications for laicisation made by priests (treatment in the interests of a law that is in any case theologically questionable). The result here is unnecessary conflict and oppressive inhumanity. And when the Congregation for the Doctrine of the Faith, writing about the pastoral care of homosexuals,[45] denies them the title of "believers in Christ" (which is always otherwise applied in such texts to baptised and confirmed Christians), then a verdict prompted by sexual morality is standing in the way of humane dealings with people belonging to a fringe group. Strictly moral Catholics then do not offer these people the congregation's help, even for the sake of ministering to HIV-infected or AIDS sufferers.

In view of what I have merely touched on here, I am unable to accept the assertion that the unlimited scope of ministry "has, for example, no direct consequences for admission

---

45 German text in: *Verlautbarungen des Apostolischen Stuhls* No. 72 (Bonn 1986).

to the Eucharist".[46] Here a dubious distinction is made between ministry and liturgy which cannot be legitimated by Jesus's own behaviour; for his Last Supper was the ultimate expression and final seal of all the previous meals he shared with sinners and those on the fringes of society, and the seal too of the ministry of them he thereby lived. This cannot be separated from the sacrament of the Eucharist, any more than the Jesus we hear about in the Gospels can be separated from the Christ of faith. It is for me too little and also considerably too wayward, to talk merely about "an analogous relationship of interdependence between charitable service and Eucharist".[47] In the context of the christological paradigm, we have rather to talk about a perichoresis – an unmingled intertwining of *Eucharist* and *diaconia*, the real presence of Christ in the sacrament and his real presence through the ministry of love in the community of Christians, and hence through the church.[48] For the risen one himself appears in strangers and the

---

46 Lehmann 'Caritas' p. 11.

47 Ibid.

48 See O. Fuchs, Die "Option für die Armen" als theologisches Prinzip für den christlichen Selbstvollzug von Individuum und Gesellschaft. In: A. Bucher e.a. (ed.), *Die "vorrangige Option für die Armen" der Katholischen Kirche in Lateinamerika*, Vol. 1 (Eichstätt 1991) pp. 32-52.

sick (cf. Mt 25,35-36), just as he is also really present, through his Spirit, in all those who help and liberate.

This interactive Christo-praxis between helpers and sufferers, the rejected and those who receive them, gives Christology in the sphere of faith and Christodoxology in the sphere of worship their all-embracing dimension – the dimension comprehending the whole of life. Faith and worship then no longer act as a blockade against unrestricted service. They are experienced as the enabling foundation and context of a service which devotes itself without ifs and buts to the underprivileged, the sick and those in need. People who believe that their whole existence is founded in God until death and beyond, *can* – out of this inexhaustible fact of God's love – give themselves to suffering men and women. Since God's love is already theirs without reserve, they can give unreserved love themselves, and spend themselves within the limits of their possibilities and the impotence they experience.

The saving universality of the Eucharist, and hence its "ministering" diaconical dimension, should therefore be maintained, at least for all baptised Christians,[49] so that in the church

49 I do not speak here of the invitation to *all* the suffering, or to all people of good will, to partake of the Eucharist, since this could also be interpreted as an

people may discover that, in its own sphere, the church deals with sinners (or those whom it seems sinners) in exactly the same way that God, in his infinite readiness for reconciliation, encounters sinners: that is, in unconditional love – not merely after they have duly changed their ways, but beforehand, so that they *can* change, within the framework of their own possibilities. God's righteousness does not set up any meritocratic conditions. He justifies sinners and the godless. All Christians have a right to a praxis of ministry in everything that happens in the church – a praxis in which grace goes before law, and where love is freed from the constraints of morality. "It is therefore theologically and pastorally atrocious to give the impression that it is not love that is the fulfilment of the law and the first of the commandments, but

appropriation of 'non-Christian' helpers or people in need. The Eucharistic celebration is a special sphere for the *koinonia* of the church, where *all Christians* can assure themselves of God's unconditional grace and love for human beings, and where, in the power of this divine Spirit, they may be encouraged to practise similar unconditional ministry towards others. But, as in the case of baptism and faith, this (restricted) sphere of participation in the sacramental life of the church, with the resources conferred there, has as its purpose the passing on of what has been received – not through the strategy of 'compelling them to come in' but in outgoing love.

144

rather complete identification with the church's doctrine of faith and morals."[50]

The different conditions in which Christians live are always fragmentary. One person lives more in the sphere of explicit faith, another more in the sphere of charitable service, again others rather in the common life of the Christian community. It is only on the basis of mutual service, and in the acceptance of mutual *limitations* that Christians can take one another seriously, and all the more so by exposing themselves to mutual criticism. The more the dimension of service is committed to be directly effective in all spheres of the church's own life and social forms, the more the church will itself internally become the social field *where service is learnt*; and it can then offer this service "outwards", to everyone, all the more effectively, and with all the more experience. In this way *koinonia* (community) becomes the foundation for the universal *diaconia* (service) of Christians and the church towards all human beings. It becomes the place where its own necessity and the necessity of others is discovered. But it is the place too for discussing helpful and liberating acts for those who need help, and for the helpers. So unless the church's pastoral ministry is service "inwards" – com-

---

50 Zerfaß 'Herausforderung' p. 343.

municating the gracious God *there*, in the church itself – it will hardly be able to provide the corresponding basic experience which is required for its ministry "outwards".

7.3 *The Priority of Service as Principle*

In all cases, and in principle, service is the essential option which determines the ordering of all other priorities. This must be the fundamental policy or programme, as long as there are people who suffer in the area to which a congregation belongs, or in its sphere of experience, or in the remote sectors about which it hears. After all, there is not likely to be a time in the history of mankind which would not present some form of suffering and disadvantage. This is, in principle, the permanent situation of this world (cf. Mt 26,11). It is therefore not merely a question of the "situational priority" of service "under particular conditions of congregational life",[51] because Christians and congregations *are*, in principle and from the outset, "the neighbour" of people in need; and they have to seek these people out, and discover where they are (cf. Lk 10,36). It is not for the person in need to force her or himself on

---

51 See Lehmann 'Caritas' p. 10.

146

the congregation's attention first of all, proving that he is their neighbour. They have to discover her or him, since they have made the fundamental existential decision that they will be the neighbours of the suffering. One cannot invest all one's energy in something or other – even if it is by no means bad in itself (liturgy and catechesis, for example) – if, close by, AIDS victims are dying a social death, and are hence not infrequently in danger of suicide. Service is not an optional subject in pastoral care. It is essential. This means that *diaconia* is not at the option of the person who has to decide, but is dependent on the really existing need itself.

But of course, if people do not make *diaconia*, or service, a principle, but speak only of "situational priority", this will easily impair the ability to perceive need and oppression, especially where the sufferers do not make themselves known, or are prevented by strategies of appeasement from crying their need aloud. Moreover it is only the fundamental priority of diaconia which will make people unerringly watchful to discern need; though here the background must be the also fundamental premise that suffering people themselves have the authority to define their situation and to plead their own cause. Recognition of this principle differentiates the explosive power of the concept of evangelization and the praxis or theology of liberation from all other theological outlines.[52] Only people who from the outset accept the fundamental priority of the suffering in their theology and spirituality will be able to perceive a specific situational priority at all; and they will avoid making the discernment of need and the discussion about active help depend (solely) on what they or others think best (unless they are the sufferers themselves, or have to do with them).

If we ask what ought to have a permanent "systematic" priority, before the merely situational priority of service, then of course (in most cases) we arrive at the answer: the proclamation of the Gospel, liturgy and worship. Yet if we look at the Jesus Christ of whom the Gospels tell, we have surely to perceive that what he says about the kingdom of God and about God himself is said pre-eminently in the context of encounters in which he has already acted, as healer; or where he has entered into dispute on behalf of the poor and despised. So recourse to this origin forces us to accept that in principle talk about God is not talk about God at all without the praxis of active ministry and

---

52 R. Zerfaß makes a similar plea for a European 'post-conciliar theology' which will view itself and realize itself contextually against the background of service for others. See Zerfaß 'Herausforderung' pp. 324, 338ff.

that the praxis of ministry is always the point at which we can and may talk about God.

This is very important, because one does not have to be explicitly affected by the Gospel before one is able to discover the needs of other people.[53] If this were not so we should have to put down any solidarity and discernment of need that is not motivated by Christianity and the church as 'optional social work' and depreciate it as something that has nothing to do with God. Certainly, many Christians acquire greater sensibility towards the perception of suffering because they have been touched by the Gospel. But on the other hand, human need touches the love and compassion of many people directly, as we are told it touched Jesus. They practise the Gospel in the world, even though the Gospel is never mentioned.

For centuries the Gospel was read by most interpreters of the church without their being touched at all in the way we have described. Much suggests that it is only the perception of need which provides the material hermeneutics[54] for reading the Gospel in such a way that

---

53 Contrary to Lehmann 'Caritas' p. 11, and also to P. Zulehner, *Das Gottesgerücht* (Düsseldorf 1987) p. 65.

54 On this 'material hermeneutics' cf. O. Fuchs, Die praktische Theologie im Paradigma biblisch-kritischer Handlungswissenschaft zur Praxis der Befreiung. In: O. Fuchs (ed.), *Theologie und Handeln* (Düsseldorf 1984) pp. 209-244.

it has to do with the real hope: that there is a
focal point in combatting necessity and oppression in the light of the kingdom of God,
because the kingdom thereby acquires reality, in
germ, in the way men and women shape their
lives. And it is this reality alone which has a
future, down to the coming of that kingdom
and into the kingdom itself. Accordingly it is
true to say that people who allow themselves to
be touched by the need of others will never
read the Gospel except with the eyes of compassion, and will discover the corresponding
faith. This will be so all the more if they encounter Christians and proclaimers of the
Gospel who place a high value on all forms of
diaconical service, and link them with talk
about God in the context of the Jewish-Christian tradition; though this link may be either
explicit, or forged through the recognition and
gift of loving service.

7.4 *The Use of Theology*

But of what use are these reflections of a
"practical theologian" in the context of the
scholarly disciples, with the diversified organization prevailing there today? R.Zerfaß does
not take a very exalted view of their usefulness,
because in his view scholarly theology is too

bookish and not contextual enough. Moreover he thinks that it is illusory for this theology to imagine that it can deepen the spiritual motivation of those concerned with it.[55] My own experience does not permit me any emphatic contradiction. And yet I am inclined not to set so little store by the reflections of university theology about service for others. After all, here a long overdue process is at last taking place within theology itself; for it is trying in its discussions to arrive at a high, argumentative theological assessment of diaconia.[56]

Apart from this clarification of the significance of service in theology's own field, I should not like to discredit the – at least possible – effect of these endeavours (an effect which is also continually experienced in the relevant encounters). For one result is that the people engaged in pastoral care and proclamation are attaching increasing importance to this kind of ministry (or at least pay it lip service). And this means greater appreciation of all those in the congregation who perform the little and the greater services, and are involved in social work. A change, step by step, in the awareness

55 See Zerfaß 'Herausforderung' pp. 324,328-339.
56 Cf. O. Fuchs, Wie verändert sich das Verständnis von Theologie, wenn die Diakonik zum Zuge kommt? In: *Pastoraltheologische Informationen 10* (1990) 25, pp. 175-202.

and spirituality of theologians (men and women) and of clergy would perhaps be a fruitful beginning – provided that one believes that awareness has to some degree genuine power.

I believe too that it is not pure illusion to hope that theologians may enter into an exchange of views, for example with social workers, and that they may pass on their ideas as motivating help to the people concerned. But this exchange must be on equal terms and in the appropriate language. And it will be the more fruitful the more theologians allow themselves to be affected by what they are told about the social field involved. Perhaps we are after all gradually rediscovering common social sectors, where theological concepts make their impact, not as indoctrination and discipline, but as ideas, which put themselves at risk in confrontation with the narratives of those engaged in charitable service, and let themselves be forged by these people's experiences and opportunities for faith.

Ultimately speaking, "contextuality" cannot be entirely denied to the theologians concerned with diaconia, because they themselves are often forced, with some anguish, to think about it, because of real experiences of personal suffering, and through the suffering of others. The reproach is of course still justified where this contextuality remains largely private, and does not enter explicitly into the publications of these theologians. That is no doubt connected with the nature of European theology, which is largely argumentative and not sufficiently "narratively" sustained. This is probably the justifiable criticism of an insufficiently contextual theology: that individual contexts are insufficiently brought into the discussion of principles, and are insufficiently accepted. That is to say, they are not sufficiently used as starting points and tend to be forgotten in subsequent reflection. Yet these individual contexts have a dignity as "arguments" of a special kind, for which rational argument is no substitute. One would often like to know even from theologians the places and starting points of their specific concern.

This would in itself be the beginning of a change in theology from professionally academic thinking to personal and positional reflections in the context of individual experiences, not merely with books but also with human life and suffering. It would mean entering the context of certain suffering people, and of corresponding projects near by, as well as entering into active and political solidarity with people far away. But certainly to achieve this, and with this in minds, theologians would courageously have to try out and discover a new language.

153

Particularly theologians belonging to the "First World" will need much conversion before they can press forward a theology which is there for other people, and which finds expression in ministry for others. But in entering on this path theology may perhaps become a driving force which – though its efficacy must not be overestimated – cannot be ignored in a Church that is constituted through service for other people.

8. Service to the Individual in a Pluralistic Community

I have already mentioned several times the necessity of plurality within the church on the basis of the freedom of the individual believers, theologically speaking, of their charismata or vocations. This subject still needs some further completeness of detail, according to the insight that the diaconical dimension also includes integrally the service to the development of the uniqueness of each individual. Not only because of his or her freedom, but also because of the fact that only people who are allowed to use their power of reason, creativity and their practical possibilities are able to realize their required diaconical tasks in an effective and innovative way.

The following chapter broaches this problem by means of a particular example of realization of the situation if theologians make use of sociological, empirical analyses. Such analyses are very important sources in "seeing" what is necessary for the liberation of people to attain their own possibilities, for the examination of apparent needs in their profile, intensity and scope and for revealing of hidden needs which are not easily discovered on the surface of daily life.

Besides, in this chapter, a realistic example can be found of whether the theologians deal with empirical materials from the perspective of a diaconical conception of the church or not (see above chapter 7.4). Is their theological impact on such results really useful in terms of the option that the church stands on the side of those who enjoy or need freedom, even if such an option shocks and endangers the (mostly boring) peacefulness and safety of the church institutions? The question here is between a diaconical or selfish organization of the church.

8.1 *Horizons of Interpretation and Interests for Action*

The empirical basis of the following contribution is confined to an article which appeared in a publication of the German "Institut für Demoskopie in Allensbach".[57] The piece written by R. Köcher bore the heading: "Religiös in einer säkularisierten Welt" (Religious in a Secularized World).[58] The particular data

---

57 E. Noelle-Neumann & R. Köcher, *Die verletzte Nation. Über den Versuch der Deutschen, ihren Charakter zu ändern* (Stuttgart 1987).

58 Ibid. pp. 164-281.

which gave rise to the following reflections,
briefly stated, are:

1) In recent decades a de-institutionalization of
   the religious has been taking place from
   which, in the long run, a strengthening of
   religion per se cannot be expected: "Whoever weakens the church undermines religiosity."[59] The origin of the de-institutionalization, and with it, the weakening of religion, lies in an "increase in the religious
   autonomy of the individual", and with it, an
   "individualization of religion".[60]

2) A weakening of the bond with the church
   fosters not only "a distancing of the relationship between generations through the
   decreasing recognition of their obligations
   to each other", but also a decreasing recognition of the obligations and responsibilities
   to the general population and its future.[61]
   "Where religion and the church are weak,
   egocentrism and hedonism gain ground,
   individual autonomy becomes the predominant goal, the pursuit of which does not
   tolerate any absolutely postulated relationships and obligations".[62]

---

59 Köcher 'Religiös' p. 184.
60 Ibid. p. 184, cf. also pp. 180ff.,197.
61 Cf. Köcher 'Religiös' pp. 194, 196.
62 Ibid. p. 197.

The following is not concerned with finding difficulties in these empirical data, and therefore also not with the possible and necessary discussion of them in the context of other studies. The central issue is rather the question concerning the relationship between description and interpretation as shown in the presentation of the results themselves, as well as, and especially in the ecclesiastical assimilation and interpretation of the results so presented. This is a critical undertaking, in which the criteria are of a theological nature. For, on one's theological framework depend also one's assessment and explanation of empirically-based statements. Different ecclesiological perspectives lead to different interpretations and from there also to different proposals for action.

Ever since the publication of the results of the investigation, they have been constantly cited in West German churches, especially by church officials, and have been regarded as authoritative in this field. This has given rise to particular complaints and postulates. The results are a cheap source for interpreting the church's situation, pastoral praxis, and their future direction.

Our question therefore is: Which interests were at work in the assimilation of the analyses and for which plan of action do they then serve as grounds? I will be dealing with only the survey results and interpretations mentioned above, and want to show how, in their use, numbers and the explanation of numbers are connected with, and can be allied with, intra-ecclesiastical interests in a most ambivalent way. This is not a question of a disregard for, or a rejection of, empirical research, but of the appropriate limitations of their scope and significance in connection with different theological interpretative frameworks. In so doing, we are approaching the difficult definition of the relation between empirical ecclesiastical sociology and theological conceptions of the church. The latter introduces the normativity of an "ideology", which furnishes the data with precise causal connections, and in the same way, develops precise strategies for action, in order to improve the ecclesiastical situation (as thus perceived). In each instance, the assessment of the situation, and the proposals for action to change this situation for the better, draw their criteria from the same source: from the respective conceptions of Christians and the church which guide knowledge and interpretation.

The interesting question, in this connection, regarding the extent to which Köcher's own interpretation of the empirical data already provokes, or even suggests, particular intra-ecclesiastical ways of assimilating the data and particular theological positions, will not be further pursued here. I will content myself with the suggestion that in the publications the interpretative framework is the result of a perspective on religion and church which supports the functional reduction of religion for the upkeep of generally accepted values of the state and society as they are, and the further suggestion that, therefore, a concept of political order is pursued which proceeds primarily from the necessary function of existing institutions and systems of obligations.[63]

8.2 *Evaluation of the Empirical Information in the Ecclesiastical Sphere*

In not a few of the proceedings of the Academy and conferences of the church, I have personally witnessed the using of the survey results which I am here subjecting to debate, especially in a perspective which could be summarized as follows: "Since there is no religion without ecclesiastical institution, this institution and its official representatives must be strengthened."[64]

---

63 Cf. Köcher 'Religiös' pp. 180ff., 197, cf. also eadem: Familie und Gesellschaft. In: Noelle-Neumann/ Köcher 'Verletzte Nation' (pp. 74-163) pp. 96ff., 103ff.

64 Compare Köcher's statement 'Whoever weakens the church, undermines religiosity." This statement sounds very favorable to restoration oriented people

In this way, *empirical* information is translated, via particular ecclesiastical *concepts* of norm, whether, directly or indirectly, into *statements* of norm. At the same time, further questions and considerations regarding content are annulled and the contents are immunized against any other possible "versions" of the material. Where, however, the possible solutions and criteria for action are sought only within the functional deficiency of the existing relations, and as integralist repairs to the existing system, there is little room for alternative content and structural innovations. Nothing then stands in the way of a neo-conservative assimilation of the empirical results, especially since it is able to surround itself with the aura of a scientific foundation, thus likewise disarming any

---

of the church, since they are here easily able to identify their hierarchical conception of the church with the institutional-sociological empirical church. Description and ideology suddenly fuse, since it is not sufficiently clear of which church we are speaking here: obviously of ecclesiastical institutions which are responsible for proclamation in word and sacrament, and which locate this proclamation in the distinction of clergy from laity. *The* church which, by way of example is present and active in society in the charitable organizations, is as little in view here as the church which arises wherever baptized people gather or live with one another (where institutional completeness and proxemity to clergy are relatively secondary).

consideration of the problems of the underlying ideology. These brief comments make it apparent how the transmission of such analysis results into the church realm is exposed to an ideological field of tension.

In the search for *alternative* interpretations, the theologian is reminded of the perception of the key statement of Vatican II, "Signs of the Time", which was as follows: Emerging situation and Christian message come into contact with each other in such a way that they enrich each other in their reciprocal responsibilities for the concrete betterment of human life and action, always with the critical contribution of the Gospel over against the situation, yet neither over and above nor against its dynamic. One condition for this, however, is an attitude which understands the current relationships and development not only as a bad world over against the good Gospel (and the church), but which also understands it as a potential coming of the Spirit of God, which "blows wherever it pleases": that is, in all that which allows human life to become freer and fuller. Then, from the church's deposit of traditions, may arise corresponding alternative models and experiments in praxis for shaping life, community, society, and not least, the church itself.

If, by way of contrast, it is correct that the church leadership is trying to react to the current tradition crisis in Christian belief with, in particular, a retrospective orientation toward traditional and existing forms of the preservation of ecclesiastical identity, then the intra-ecclesiastical reasons for it could lie in the tendency within the church organization to regard innovations as *disturbances*. Obviously, one cannot imagine a church institution which *needs* changes corresponding to its own (also institutional!) identity. Under the motto, imitation of Christ, challenges and radical claims not infrequently find their premature limits at the point where the authority of the church in its existing social and institutional form, as well as in the economic and political entanglements connected with it, is questioned. The tradition crisis appears, from this perspective, at least *in part*, to be a crisis of the continuity of the church itself, in so far it is not sufficiently able, creatively and openly, to bring the recurrent newness of its own message into contact with more recent contemporary developments. The rejection of the innovative potentials of the age is not an expression of its critique, but the refusal of a critical encounter via a regressive escapist reaction. The internal-ecclesiastical result of such a strategy by the church leadership and its exponents is that proper belief is collectivistically demanded, especially in the form of confession-oriented consent and morally good conduct (especially in the area of sexual morals).

In what follows, an attempt is made to find alternative, theologically justifiable interpretations of the empirical data before us, and then also to arrive at other proposals for action for a future ecclesiastical self-fulfilment. This can be done here only briefly. In terms of church politics, we are dealing here with a long overdue corrective to the one-dimensional way in which, for a long time now, empirical information has been generally assimilated and applied to the intra-ecclesiastical debate.

The following general insight may be relevant beyond this particular example. Because generally the results of empirical research end up, within the church, in theological conflicts and inner-ecclesiastical debates (especially those surrounding the authentic interpretation and implementation of Vatican II). The meaning and importance of empirical information are also primarily measured by the respective opponents in terms of its status and value within the current debate. Crucial to this is that each of the different theological and church-political interpretations is not offered as containing empirical facts and is therefore not furnished with the dignity of a contradiction-resistent argument; rather, the theological motives themselves, including the problems they produce in *theological* discourse, are exposed, laid bare, and discussed in detachment from, as well as closeness to, the empirical data.

8.3 *Individuality and Plurality as Challenges to the Church's Community*

The research results emphatically underline the fact that a de-institutionalization of the Christian religion should be resisted. The question however, the answer to which depends on the interpretation of this statement, is this: To which structural model should and must an ecclesiastical institution turn itself when it exposes itself to the responsibility of the Gospel for concrete historical reality, reacts to it, and at the same time accordingly transforms it? If it is the case that "the church has only sporadic or no direct contact with the majority of its members; this means an profound failure of the system of communication...",[65] then one must not find the cause of that failure in the fact that the old structural and communication model ("top to bottom") no longer functions, rather one could probably more accurately find the cause of this failure in the fact that precisely this old model is *still* functioning and is required to

---

65 Köcher 'Religiös' p. 182.

function, and therefore is not able to react to the altered social relations and the potential contributions to humanization lying within them. Whether one is inclined to one interpretation or another, is already a question of theology, which derives from people and the church.

Those who (especially in the church leadership) generally adhere only to a *hierarchological* system of the church, in which church attendance, preaching of the ministers, and total identification with the church credo and with the moral ideas of the church form the dominant concept of the institution, exercise a strategy which can hardly positively accept the tendency described as "individualization". This recourse to the old integralist problem-solving models carries with it the danger of weakening the capability of constructive interchange with the surrounding world, while also encouraging a "ghettoization" of the church. In the long run, this interpretation and course of action can even show itself to be highly destructive for this institution. Thus claims Ch.Duquoc: "The church, however, drives into schizophrenia. For on the one hand, it fosters creative responsibility in the world; on the other hand, however, it forces one towards antiquated ethical and disciplinary modes of conduct, by its refusal of a democratic debate over that which con-

166

cerns all the baptized."[66] With such an interpretation one will hardly be able to disclose the
ecclesiogenic share of the guilt for the relationships which are now the object of complaint.

I see alternative models of interpretation and
problem-solving especially in the Charismatic
Theology and People-of-God-Theology of
Vatican II. From such a *pneumatological* view of
the church, the so-called individualization
could be, considered an advance and an
opportunity, in the sense of the "signs of the
time", also as an opportunity to trace the intra-
ecclesiastical causes of the individualist move-
ment away from the church institution (as, for
example, they are to be found in the authoritar-
ian and indoctrinating modes of conduct, which
leave no room for the freedom and charisma of
the individual). From this line of approach what
would matter would be to take the individual
seriously and to allow communicative networks
to arise which make possible another index of
order, namely, one of an equal unity of all
believers in their *diversity*.[67] When plurality, as
an integral element of the structure of the
church, is not only permitted, but is increasingly considered to be its wealth, the religious

---

66 Ch. Duquoc, Kirchenzugehörigkeit und christliche
    Identität. In: *Concilium 24* (1988) p. 168.
67 Cf. in detail O.Fuchs, *Zwischen Wahrhaftigkeit und
    Macht* (Frankfurt/M. 1990).

autonomy of man is bound to relational fields which do not destroy this autonomy, but creatively develop it *and* at the same time put limits on it. Precisely for that reason, the freedom of the individual must not be kept out of the church because it might lead to the destruction of the institution, for it could even develop and help to structure this church and its institutions (which would then, of course, look different). In this way a new, and perhaps the best, possibility opens up for preventing *false* individualization and isolation, since people are here *granted individually* without having to *renounce the community*.

By way of contrast, a restorative approach to the church drives out the devil by Beelzebul, since it fails to make use of this available resource for community and institution formation, and in so doing, turns itself into a ghetto. Precisely when the church tries to achieve integration and institutional preservation by means of the old structural model, it cannot prevent itself from being excluded and defined by the advancing wake of technological functionalization.[68] The church can then only, and not ulti-

---

68 To this exclusion corresponds the area-specific circumscription of the church and religion and, not least, of the spiritual sciences to the compensating function of what which cannot be rationalized. In so doing, a constructive and critical role over against the

mately, "reach" into all areas of society as an *institution*, if it no longer (simply) "straight-jackets" the individual in prescribed institutional role assignments, but reconstitutes *itself on the basis of* "the *release* of the individual for decision-making in the choice of his specific role combinations".[69] "The emancipation of the individual decision has as its consequence that the participation motives are not completely controllable by the system; the subsystem must accordingly keep itself open to changes in the situation of the individual motive".[70] What has always been a problem, not only for ecclesiastical institutions, namely, spelling out at the same time individual freedom *and* membership in the community, becomes henceforth the problem of the survival of the institution per se.

---

functionalized areas of life and work is granted neither to the spiritual sciences, nor to religion, nor to its dependencies (universities and churches). On the problematic neo-conservative defense of the spiritual sciences in the category of cultural compensation and crisis reparation, see H.Schnädelbach, Kritik der Kompensation. In: *Kursbuch 91* (1988) pp. 35-45.

69 K. Gabriel, Nachchristliche Gesellschaft heute! Christentum und Kirche vor der entfalteten Moderne. In: *Diakonia 19* (1988) pp. 27-34, 33.

70 Ibid. pp. 33-34.

8.4 *The Individual and the Connection of the Church to the World*

With a *positive* acceptance of the increasing degree of individualization in the ecclesiastical social structures, the danger of an area-specific reduction of the overall claim of the Christian message and of ecclesiastical existence (over against society and world) is properly dealt with and counteracted, in that free Christians, in their societal engagement, neither allow themselves to be limited by the church to the protection of the right to life of the unborn, nor accept from society, sanctions on its critical position with respect to the environment, the military, or the economy. Whoever ventures to make use of his or her freedom *in* belief within the community will also be able outside the church to act upon the freedom of his or her Christian options in all possible and necessary areas with appropriate support and with all the more civil courage.

Köcher also sees in the area-specific reduction of the worldly mission of the church to the internal religious and liturgical areas in the narrow sense, a great danger of weakening its institution.[71] Such a reduction has certainly not already been remedied through courageously

---

71 Cf. Köcher 'Religiös' pp. 182ff.

externalizing such intra-ecclesiastically valid signs of membership (church attendance, saying grace, Catholic confession, religious forms of expression etc.) and courageously and valiantly carrying them out within, and in contradistinction to, the secular spheres of life (as, for example, the individual Catholic saying grace on the periphery of a restaurant). For such externalized signs of church membership (in which one concentrates on the decisive connection with the world) often also strengthen the loss of wordly responsibility in the social and political contexts of life which lie beyond these. Obviously, such contexts must themselves arise and be thematized via individual subjects and their experiences in the church, so that they can also be taken place outside the church and carried out by Christians.

The answer, therefore, to that which makes up the Christian "service to the world", depends once again on the various conceptions of the church. The one sees the church as primarily a place of liturgical and religious confession, whose connection to the world finds expression primarily when one confesses to the world his or her membership via the appropriate signs. The other can be found especially in the theology of vocation of Vatican II, as well as in the concept of evangelization of the teaching office (cf. EN), in that evangelization concerns not only the liturgical and religious area, but extends to all areas of human life and society; and also in that this should not be considered and realized without the equal calling of all Christians to reciprocal evangelism in this sense. Here has stood, therefore, already for a long time now, a concept of the content of ecclesiastical service in and to the world, which is able to structure the relationship between individual Christian maturity and ecclesiastical opportunities for participation in the formation of the world in reciprocally increasing proportionality.

Distinctive ecclesiastical structural models are here involved. The first conception gives preference to the structural model of the authoritative transmission of knowledge of life and faith through a clergy which claims, in cultus and word, the exclusive competence and authority for the valid mediation of salvation. The second concept prefers a structural model which proceeds in principle from the equality of all gifts among the people of God, and obliges the ecclesiastical office to ensure that Christians, with their own experiences, understanding, and proposals for action, also really have importance within the church's social patterns, and mutually enrich, criticize, and complement each other there.

In this connection, one should remember the empirical insight that a minority of church-oriented Christians remove from public view and privatize their religious forms of expression and content, since they hardly occur in social life, and are considered alien elements. Such Christian "speak less of their convictions, and likewise are silent with reference to what they consider to be important".[72] Immediately within the predominant hierarchical-authoritative structural model the ecclesiastical side responds to this fact with the postulation of the "service to the world" of the laity, which consists of also confessing on the "outside" the faith received in ecclesiastically mediated salvation. What is little considered here is that they are demanding something for which they scarcely permit one to be equipped within the church. For within the church, there are no structural opportunities for the laity to speak of their experiences with God, people, and the church, and to mutually limit and upbuild one another in their diversity and partiality (uncensored by the clergy's "theological" claims to unabridgement). Especially within the church there are too few fields of experience in which Christians can be aware of the importance of their own belief for the *public* belief of the church. Therefore, what Köcher, with reference to the dilemma of the church-

---

72 Cf. R. Köcher, Die Entwicklung von Religiosität und Kirchlichkeit. In: *Diakonia 19* (1988) pp. 35-39, p. 37.

oriented societal minority, attributes to external factors, is in fact the intra-ecclesiastical dilemma itself: the laity have little opportunity to speak about their own convictions and are already silent with regard to that which is important to them from their own life experience.

Ultimately the reason for this is that a minority of non-church-oriented *Christians* increasingly remove themselves from the existing social patterns of the church, without losing their own Christian self-understanding and also continually with the claim to be able, instead, to restore the concept of the church for themselves. Here we are primarily dealing with people for whom it is not (only) a question of the form of expression of belief, but who also design and pursue appropriate social initiatives and forms of action which express solidarity, such as difficult (party) political choices. In this direction, a progressive dynamic could be underway, future developments of which cannot be foreseen. In any case, we are dealing here, by their own claim, not with Christians who are far from the church but with those who for the sake of evangelism distance themselves from ecclesiastical institutions and realize their own ecclesiastical self-fulfilment in the "proximate" (in completely new structural forms). Here looms an *actual*, markedly contrasting juxtaposition with the structural model

174

which had until now only been conceived of.
Also, according to Köcher, "a minority [is]...
seldom about the church, and nevertheless
tightly bound to the Christian faith".[73]

In explanation of the tension within these
intra-ecclesiastical relations separate empirical
studies should have been set up which do not a
priori interpret distance from the church as a
weakening of the institution, but which proceed
from the preconception that the minority referred to is at present constantly growing and is
developing other new institutional structures, so
that they do not weaken the institution per se
but rather merely *the existing* institutional conditions of the church, about which it is not asked
and from which it is itself excluded. Perhaps,
from such studies then, would appear distinctive
insights into the basis of the Christian-motivat-
ed critique of the church and church-farness
(from existing ecclesiastical institutions), as well
as into their analysis and their own structural
self-fulfilment. In any case, 58% of those who
have little or no confidence in the church describe themselves as religious. And 33 % of these
"church-far", who lack confidence in the
church, draw strength and comfort from the
faith.[74]

---

73 Köcher 'Religiös' p. 163, cf.184.
74 Cf. Köcher 'Religiös' p. 241.

8.5 Prospect

These investigations show that what is lamented or welcomed as the "de-churching" or "re-churching" of Christianity or Christians, always depends on the theological framework, as well as on the organizational structural model, which is associated with the concept of church. Arising here, in interpretation and realization, are important inner-ecclesiastical decisions. Since the church has more dismissed than dealt with the claim of contemporary modernity with regard to the "re-churching" of Christianity, through multiple institutional straight-jackets and the binding of its members to the institutional environment, as well as through an innovation-shy, discursive organization of theology.[75] At the threshold of the post-Christian era, or post-modernity,[76] in my opinion, the epochal decision has to be made to conceive of and fashion the future self-realization of the

---

75 Cf. Gabriel 'Nachchristliche Gesellschaft' pp. 30ff.; R.Bucher, Die Theologie, das Fremde. Der Theologische Diskurs und sein anderes. In: O. Fuchs (ed.) *Die Fremden* (Düsseldorf 1988) pp. 302-319, pp. 309ff.

76 Cf. W. Welsch, Vielheit ohne Einheit? Zum gegenwärtigen Spektrum der philosophischen Diskussion um die 'Postmoderne'. In: *Philosophisches Jahrbuch 94* (1987) pp. 111-141, pp. 139ff.

church *not in opposition to* the advancing individalization of the people, but *with it.* Between the above-mentioned different, and partially opposing, frameworks of interpretation for the empirical facts presented, I myself vote, not least on theological grounds, for the alternative. Then future church formation does not "ghettoize" itself beyond the historical situation, but involves itself critically and participatively in social circumstances and conditions, by accepting the perspective, both in principle and in fact, of the plurality and difference of all people. It also takes upon itself the developing communicative responsibility, which becomes productive precisely in this perspective, by permitting, promoting and structuring unity-enhancing transitions, connections and contacts, which do not centralistically destroy the diversity, but produce fruit as a real facilitating basis of unity.

In direct accordance with the theology of Vatican II, being attentive to historical trends cannot only be harmonized with the content of the Gospel, but can also actually provoke certain starting-points for evangelization which have until now been little realized, and in so doing can even deepen and enrich the identity of the church. This does not prevent the critical debate with extreme tendencies toward individualization and with the "fanatical take-oneself-seriously groups".[77] Since this necessary debate is not carried out against human individuality and at its expense, but with it, and especially, with the individual subjects themselves, for, it is precisely the latter which makes possible *that* communication which allows the limits of individualization to be found and definitely not through restorative, ultimately alienating hierarchicalization, but rather through structural openness to mutual critique and delimitation of the individual by the individuality of others.[78]

Not only in order to combat the "absolute dissolution of reason", but also to combat the dissolution of the Church, "we do not, however, have to rely on vertical control, it can also be checked through lateral forms of interchange. A network of heterogenious, yet variously intertwined, not only mutually-exclusive, but also mutually-overlapping, fields of rationality, discourses, life-forms, and life-worlds, would have many intersections, transition points, possibilities for translation, and conflict zones, but no standard mid-point or vanishing-point".[79] This statement of the phi-

---

77 Köcher 'Religiös' p. 196.
78 Cf. O. Fuchs, Narrativität und Widerspenstigkeit. In: R. Zerfaß (ed.), *Erzählter Glaube – Erzählende Kirche* (Freiburg 1988) pp. 87-123.
79 B. Waldenfels, *In den Netzen der Lebenswelt* (Frankfurt 1985) p. 117.

losopher corresponds well with the ecclesiastical statement of the theologian: "The church is a church of the Spirit of the infinite and incomprehensible God, whose blessed unity can only be broken into so many different mirrors in this world, whose ultimate satisfying unity is only God Himself, or else nothing".[80] The goal here is the strengthening of the subject for mutual communal maturity in equality and diversity.

---

80 K. Rahner, Rede des Ignatius von Loyola an einen Jesuiten von Heute. In: K. Rahner/P. Imhof, *Ignatius von Loyola* (Freiburg 1978) p. 28.